For Narda

and for

FIGHTING
WORDS !!

Robin Morgan

ALSO BY ROBIN MORGAN

Poetry

A Hot January: Poems 1996–1999
Upstairs in the Garden: Selected and New Poems
Depth Perception
Death Benefits
Lady of the Beasts
Monster
Fiction
The Burning Time
Dry Your Smile
The Mer Child
The Handmaiden of the Holy Man

Nonfiction

Saturday's Child: A Memoir
The Word of a Woman
The Demon Lover: The Roots of Terrorism
A Woman's Creed
The Anatomy of Freedom
Going Too Far

Anthologies

(compiled, edited, and introduced)
Sisterhood Is Forever
Sisterhood Is Global
Sisterhood Is Powerful
The New Woman (co-ed.)

FIGHTING
WORDS

A TOOLKIT FOR COMBATING
THE RELIGIOUS RIGHT

ROBIN MORGAN

NATION BOOKS
NEW YORK

For Suzanne Braun Levine

and

Bob Levine

FIGHTING WORDS
A Toolkit for Combating the Religious Rights

Published by
Nation Books
An Imprint of Avalon Publishing Group, Inc.
245 West 17th Street, 11th Floor
New York, NY 10011

AVALON
publishing group incorporated

Nation Books is a co-publishing venture of the Nation Institute and Avalon
Publishing Group Incorporated.

Library of Congress Cataloging-in-Publication Data

ISBN-10: 1-56025-948-5
ISBN-13: 978-1-56025-948-0

9 8 7 6 5 4 3 2 1

Book design by Maria E. Torres

Printed in the United States of America
Distributed by Publishers Group West

Contents

Introduction

It Is Happening Here

Are you muttering to yourself a lot lately? Do you gnash your teeth, shout at your TV set, compare incredulous notes with friends? Do you try to laugh at it all, or deal with it by sending a check to an organization? Do you feel yourself wearying from the dogged assaults of our homegrown American Taliban; chafing at cynical, political manipulations of personal faith; or hardening with indifference at the familiarity of Orwellian double-speak? (My favorite for today is Senator Orrin Hatch's "Capital punishment is our society's recognition of the sanctity of human life.")

Do you feel helpless, as it keeps getting worse?

As I write this, in May 2006, it no longer seems such a mystery that Europe's Dark Ages could affirm superstitions that empowered the church while eradicating knowledge of how to build aqueducts, trepan skulls for brain surgery, safely deliver or abort a pregnancy, construct indoor plumbing, practice sophisticated herbal medicine, or even simply read and write.

Today, science in the United States—once a world leader in virtually every research field—is under intense assault from the extreme religious right, via its White House representative, President George W. Bush. No matter how vast the scientific consensus that fossil fuels constitute a principal factor in climate change, Bush's administration still won't sign the Kyoto Protocol (and still speaks longingly of oil-drilling in the Alaskan wilderness). In 2006, the National Institutes of Health budget is being cut—for the first time in thirty-six years. The United States now educates fewer scientists each year, and now imports more high-tech products than it exports. Bush administration policy dictates that one-third of all government HIV-prevention spending—hundreds of millions—must go to "abstinence until marriage" programs, while government funding for programs that support condom use have been eviscerated (this, despite the failure rate for abstinence programs proving many times higher than for condom use). The Federal Drug Administration and the Centers for Disease Control (CDC) have both been forced to take positions that please religious conservatives despite being contrary to their own scientific findings—on the "morning after" Plan B pill and on condom use—provoking public resignations of scientists from both federal agencies. Reginald Finger, an evangelical Focus on the Family member and Bush appointee to the CDC Immunization Committee, says he might actually oppose an HIV vaccine if one becomes available: "With any vaccine for HIV, dis-inhibition [freedom from fear, presumably of sex] would certainly be a factor and it is something we will have to pay attention to." Finger may even block approval for a vaccine protecting women against HPV, the human papilloma virus that can cause cancer of the cervix. He worries, "This vaccine may be sending an overall message to teenagers that 'We expect you to be sexually active.'" Meanwhile, the administration sends antichoice lobbyists as delegates to international meetings on women's health, and pressures global conferences on AIDS to have Reverend Franklin Graham lecture on "faith-based solutions to AIDS." The religious right's effect on Bush's opposition to stem-cell research is notorious, despite the majority of scientists—and U.S. citizens, *including* evangelicals—supporting research that potentially could have as massive an impact on health as antibiotics did, particularly affecting research on cancer, Parkinson's disease, other neurological disorders, diabetes, and paralysis.

The Dark Ages indeed. With the Crusades thrown in, to boot.

Recently, news coverage has been focused on worldwide marches, boycotts, flag- and building-burnings by Muslims protesting cartoons that allegedly mocked the Prophet Muhammad, run by a Danish newspaper last year. TV pundits tsk-tsk about these "obsessed fanatics," these literalist, fundamentalist extremists, while commentators (and U.S. politicians) discover a seemingly newfound pride in "Western free speech." OK. Fair enough. All right.

But meanwhile, little attention is given to a short item running in only a few newspapers on February 11: protests by Callaway Christian Church members in Fulton, Missouri, which resulted in cancellation of the scheduled high-school spring production of Arthur Miller's American classic, *The Crucible*. The Christian protests were actually about the high school having *already* staged a (considerably tamed) version of the musical *Grease*—yes, honest, that depraved orgy, *Grease*—but their chilling effect was sufficient for Mark Ederle, superintendent of schools, to ban the Miller play, thus saving the school from being further "mired in controversy." The drama teacher, Wendy DeVore, quit after learning that her contract would almost certainly not be renewed. Dr. Ederle said, "That was me in my worst Joe McCarthy moment, to some." Since Miller intended *The Crucible*, set in Salem, Massachusetts, during the witch trials, as a metaphor *for* McCarthyism, well, Dr. Ederle . . . yes.

Not one news commentator pointed out the parallels, wondered why free speech was such a great idea to brandish abroad but not at home, or compared one set of obsessed, fanatic, literalist, fundamentalist extremists against freedom of expression with the other.

On August 15, 1997, a man named Gil Alexander-Moegerle held a press conference in Colorado Springs. Cofounder with James Dobson of the group Focus on the Family, he had just authored a book, *James Dobson's War on America*, the first insider expose of a major religious-right organization. Amazingly, Alexander-Moegerle, taking his Christianity seriously for a change, offered a public apology to all women, men of color, Jews, Muslims, homosexual people, and others harmed by "actions and attitudes on the part of the Christian Right in general and James Dobson and Focus on the Family in particular." He also revealed how corruptly the Christian right operates behind the scenes, urged an end to political lobbying by such organizations, and issued a warning to the American people. There was virtually no coverage of his press conference (though it is still available in full at www.ralliance.org/Alexander-Moegerle.html). His book was barely reviewed.

Even our media is afraid. Our media's corporate ownership is afraid.

We are all more than a little afraid.

And we are tired.

The great Supreme Court Justice Louis D. Brandeis wrote, "Those who won our independence believed . . . that the greatest menace to freedom is an inert people. . . . that it is hazardous to discourage thought, hope, and imagination; that fear breeds repression; that repression breeds hate; that hate menaces stable government. . . . [Fear] cannot alone justify suppression of free speech and assembly. Men feared witches and burnt women. It is the function of speech to free men from the bondage of irrational fears" (Concurrence in *Whitney v. California*, 1927).

But really, should we be surprised that the state of the Union has been corroded this far, or that religion should be employed as the corrosive element?

After all, God is always claimed by both sides in every war, and the Bible has been used to defend the Crusades, the Inquisitions, conquest, slavery, lynching, apartheid, indentured servitude, racism, poverty, wife battery, child abuse, homophobia, and other holy terrors.

After all, the decade 1991–2001 saw multiple attacks on U.S. clinics and medical personnel providing contraception and abortion services, leaving 8 dead and 33 seriously wounded. Additionally, there have been more than 20 arsons and attempted arsons, 10 bombings and attempted bombings, and multiple clinics in 23 states have received threats of anthrax and chemical attacks. This was *not* called "terrorism." Yet in the wake of the September 11, 2001, attacks, the American Life League (a lay Catholic organization) ran an ad attacking Planned Parenthood in the *Washington Times*, declaring "Abortion is the ultimate terrorism."

After all, news items like the following have now become commonplace:

- The three largest Christian-right organizations call for "crusaders" to pray that certain U.S. Supreme Court justices whose voting records they dislike will die.
- Televangelist Pat Robertson blames Emmy Awards–host Ellen Degeneres for the Hurricane

Katrina disaster: "This is the second time [9/11] God has invoked a disaster before lesbian Ellen Degenerate hosted the Emmy Awards. . . . America is waiting for her to apologize for the death and destruction her sexual deviance has brought onto this great nation." Robertson also noted that the Christian Broadcasting Network had compiled a list of 283 nominees, presenters, and invited guests at the Emmys "known to be of sexually deviant persuasions."

• Citing "religious reasons," some pharmacists now refuse to fill prescriptions for emergency "morning after" contraception, flatly (and illegally) turning away their female customers— including survivors of sexual assault.

• Air Force Captain Melinda Morton, a Lutheran executive chaplain at the Air Force Academy in Colorado, resigns her commission after being fired for whistle-blowing about "strident evangelicalism" infecting the religious climate at the Academy, where fifty-five complaints about religious discrimination have been lodged in the past four years. "Evangelicalism is the official religion of the U.S. Air Force Academy," Morton warns. (And yes, this *is* the same Academy infamous for its epidemic of rape and sexual-harassment charges by female cadets—who were ignored or even *punished* for complaining.)

- Pennsylvania, Ohio, and Kansas garner some press attention for their legal battles and school board struggles over the campaign to teach "intelligent design"—"creationism" renamed—as science. But The National Center for Science Education (www.natcensied.org), which defends the teaching of evolution in public schools, notes that such battles are *increasing* in Alabama, Michigan, Mississippi, Oklahoma, Utah, and other states.

- Georgia has taken things even further— becoming the first state to approve the use of the Bible as a public school core textbook. Alabama and Missouri are looking into similar measures.

- "Faith-based prisons" are proliferating—apparently as much to rake in profits as to spread the Gospel to a captive audience. Taxpayers unwittingly finance such proselytizing prisons, where inmates receive special privileges if they follow all-day, all-week, Christian agendas. Former convicted Watergate conspirator Charles Colson's Prison Ministry Fellowship runs "partnership" prisons with its $46 million annual budget. When he was governor, George W. Bush helped launch the "Inner Change Freedom Initiative" in Texas; Inner Change now also runs prisons in Kansas and Minnesota. Another Bush governor, Jeb, happily supports three (with more to come) "faith-based prisons" in Florida. In New Mexico,

the state contracts with the Corrections Corpora-
tion of America, the largest private prison
"provider": workbooks for women prisoners
emphasize obedience under such headings as
"Yielding Rights" and "Proper Submission."

Meanwhile, the Bush administration initiates or supports:

- Providing funds for "faith-based" social-service
  programs to practice religious discrimination
  and to hire only staff who belong to the same
  church
- A school voucher program, which would give
  parents federal tax dollars for tuition to private,
  religious schools
- Pressuring staff in the White House, Justice
  Department, and other federal agencies to begin
  their workday with attendance at "voluntary"
  Bible study and prayer sessions
- Approval of a federally funded health plan for
  Catholics only, which excludes insurance coverage for contraceptives, abortion, sterilization,
  or artificial insemination
- Instituting a "religious test" for judges, promising
  to appoint only "commonsense judges who understand that our rights were derived from God."

Americans who revere the Constitution of the United
States and believe in the strict separation of religion and

government are in a state of deepening shock and growing anxiety. They include religiously observant people of every faith, as well as agnostics and atheists. Most Americans fear, sensibly, that the ultra-conservative religious right is gaining historic political power via a glib, well-organized, media-savvy movement with powerful friends in high places.

But average Americans feel helpless to confront them. Most of us haven't read the Founding Documents since grade school (if then). We assume that U.S. law has Judeo-Christian roots. (It doesn't.)

Most Americans lack the tools to argue against the religious right.

This book is the toolkit for arguing.

We don't know that *the Constitution contains not one reference to a deity*—on purpose.

We don't know that Jefferson's original draft of the Declaration of Independence *did not mention "endowed by the Creator,"* but read, "We hold these truths to be sacred and undeniable, that all men are created equal and independent; that from that equal creation they derive in rights inherent and unalienable, among which are the preservation of life, and liberty and the pursuit of happiness. . . ."

One tool in this kit is the lie detector. For instance:

- Former Attorney General John Ashcroft invoked "the Christian Fathers of our country," but actually, the Founders were a hodgepodge of freethinkers, Deists, agnostics, Christians, atheists, and Freemasons—and they were *radicals*. For example:

Question with boldness even the existence of a god. —Thomas Jefferson

Religious bondage shackles and debilitates the mind. —James Madison

I doubt of Revelation itself.—Benjamin Franklin

My own mind is my church.—Thomas Paine

- Pat Robertson claims that "In God We Trust" was on our currency and "Under God" was the U.S. motto "from 1776." Are you surprised to learn that neither was the case—until the *1950s*?
- George W. Bush adds "so help me God" to his presidential oath of office. Did he know he was defying the Constitution?
- General William Boykin, undersecretary of defense, announces, "We're a Christian nation." But the U.S. Treaty of Tripoli—initiated by George Washington and signed into law by John Adams—declares, *"The government of the United States of America is not in any sense founded on the Christian Religion."*

- Prayer circles proliferate in the U.S. House of Representatives and the Senate. Yet James Madison, "father of the Constitution," denounced the presence of *chaplains* in Congress —and even in the armed forces—as unconstitutional.

- Cardinal Egan is a front-row guest when, for the first time in history, an American president signs a bill outlawing an approved medical procedure (emergency late-term abortion). Most people believe the Roman Catholic Church's position on abortion is 2000 years old and infallible. Yet the fifteenth-century church considered abortion *moral*—and even today the prohibition is not governed by papal infallibility.

- When President George W. Bush established an "Office for Faith-Based Initiatives" inside the White House, he was in clear violation of the Lemon Test, based on a 1971 U.S. Supreme Court decision, which begins: *"Any statute [or public policy] must have a secular legislative purpose"*—and then continues with even stronger wording.

- Supreme Court Justice Antonin Scalia says, "The Constitution I interpret is not living but dead." Yet Thomas Jefferson wrote to James Madison in 1789, "[N]o society can make a perpetual constitution, or even a perpetual law. The earth belongs always to the living generation."

- Reverend Jerry Falwell blames the 9/11 attacks

on "the pagans, abortionists, feminists, gays and lesbians . . . [and other] groups who have tried to secularize America." He's a bit late: Alexander Hamilton attacked Jefferson and the other Founders for their successful *"conspiracy to establish atheism on the ruins of Christianity"* in the newly formed United States of America.

- Alabama State Supreme Court (deposed) Chief Justice Roy Moore defends his display of the Ten Commandments by claiming that U.S. law is founded on common law, in turn based on Judeo-Christian tradition. But hear this: *"We may safely affirm (though contradicted by all the judges and writers on earth) that Christianity neither is, nor ever was, a part of the common law."*— Thomas Jefferson.

The principle of separation of church and state was first articulated by Roger Williams, who was banished from Massachusetts for his beliefs and who then founded the settlement of Rhode Island in the 1600s. The Framers of the U.S. Constitution adopted this principle (and were also influenced by The Iroquois Confederacy's laws on the rights of all peoples). It has been upheld by every Supreme Court since 1879—until 2002, when the court approved school vouchers.

Now—no hyperbole—it is in genuine danger.

The United States, still a young country with a short

memory, has been swept by religious revivals before. For
instance, we now take it for granted that churches, tem-
ples, mosques, and other religious institutions are tax
exempt—but it was not always that way, nor was it the
intent of the Founders. This policy was the fruit of a religious campaign. So was "In God We Trust" getting
stamped onto our coinage, and the insertion of "Under
God" in our Pledge of Allegiance. Beginning with Lincoln's administration, presidents (and also congresses)
have repeatedly turned back attempts to pass a "Christian
Amendment" which would declare Jesus Christ "the
Ruler among nations." (Why aren't we taught this sort
of thing in school?) It's been more than eighty years
since the 1925 Scopes "Monkey" Trial in Tennessee—
where the judge wouldn't permit Clarence Darrow to
put scientists on the stand as witnesses to vouch for
Darwin's scientific method. Yet when left up to the states
(post-*Scopes*), ruling after ruling continued to ban the
teaching of evolution: *by 1930, 70 percent of U.S. school
districts did not teach evolution.* It was not until 1968, in
Epperson v. Arkansas, that the Supreme Court ruled
against such bans as having a primary religious purpose,
thus violating the Constitution's Establishment Clause.
In 1987, in *Edwards v. Aguillard*, the court used the same
rationale to strike down a Louisiana law requiring
biology teachers who taught evolution to discuss "evidence" supporting "creation science." (Moral: we can
recover from these assaults.)

Interestingly, a recent study by evolutionary scientist

Gregory Paul in the *Journal of Religion and Society* (Vol. 7, 2005) found that greater degrees of social dysfunction in a society correlated with higher religiosity. Contrary to religionists' claims that secularism produces moral decay, secular societies—for example, France, the Scandinavian countries, Japan—have far lower rates of homicide, sexually transmitted diseases, teen pregnancy, and abortion than does the United States with its high rate of religionists, a rate unique among industrialized Western nations. Similarly, the more secular "blue states" in the U.S. have lower rates of divorce, infant mortality, homicide, and violence than the so-called "red states" where fundamentalism claims to have made its beachhead.

But this religious revival, this time, is different.

What's different this time is the blatant *political* mobilization of extreme right religious forces—which in this country are primarily though not exclusively Christian—with the stated theocratic goal sometimes called "Dominionism": taking over the government and "Christianizing America." (Never mind the anguished embarrassment this causes principled Christian Americans, and never mind that such politicking contradicts Jesus' purported own words: "The kingdom of heaven is within you" [IB. IV (1904), no. 654, *The Oxyrhynchus Papyri*, 1989].

What's different this time is that the current, tightly organized, well-financed mobilization has been carefully constructed over twenty-five years, precisely to such an end.

What's different this time is that this religious extremism—peopled by scared, loyal, true believers, but led by ambitious, hypocritical, political cynics—has in fact seized power in all three branches of our government, yet wants still more.

But to *fully* grasp what's different this time, we need to pause for a brief historical aside. We've all heard religious condemnation of atheists and agnostics (along with liberals and feminists, of course) as "Nazi baby-killers" for defending a woman's right to self-determination over her own body, and how anyone who insists on strict separation of church and state is an "anti-Christian godless Nazi."

So it's crucial to understand—with history, not histrionics—just who is repeating which past, and who is not.

Adolf Hitler and the National Socialist Party came to power via coalition with and support from Germany's Christian churches, both Catholic and Protestant. Hitler, born into the Roman Catholic Church, was never excommunicated, and he forged political Concordats with the church. As late as 1941, he told one of his generals, Gerhard Engel, "I am now as before a Catholic, and will always remain so." Early in his power-consolidation, on July 14, 1933, Hitler signed into law Article 1 of the "Decree Concerning the Constitution of the German Protestant Church," merging the German Protestant Church into the Reich, and giving the Reich authority to ordain priests. Article 3 of the decree assured the new State Church that the Reich would *finance* it, stating, "Should the competent agencies of a State Church refuse to include assessments of the German Protestant Church in their budget, the appropriate State Government will cause the expenditures to be included in the budget upon request of the Reich Cabinet." The constitution of this new, state-sponsored, German church began, "At a time in which our German people are experiencing a great historical new era through the grace of God, [this church] federates into a solemn league all denominations that stem from the Reformation . . . and thereby bears witness to: 'One Body and One Spirit, One Lord, One Faith, One Baptism, One God and Father of All of Us, who is Above All, and Through All, and In All.'" Article 5 established a head for the new State Church: "Reich Bishop." Hitler appointed Ludwig Müller, a Lutheran pastor who retained the position until he committed suicide at the war's end (for more information, see www.commondreams.org).

Women—the canaries in the mine—were hit first. The *Kinder, Kirche, Kuche* ("children, church, kitchen") ideal was promulgated by the State Church, women's groups and publications were shut down, and in the year Hitler became chancellor, feminists and "non-Aryans" were forced out of jobs in education, political office, and the judiciary. In 1934, *based on religious arguments*, abortion for "Christian Aryan" women was banned and made a criminal offense against the state, punishable by hard labor or the death penalty.

Well. But surely it's different in the here and now.

There are token women, even of color, in the U.S. administration—although the reins of deep power remain clutched in rich, pale, male hands. Besides, we are the country that gave the world Madison Avenue advertising techniques—so totalitarianism here was always bound to have a slick, palatable, happy-face, *salable* veneer.

But here are some real comparison quotes.

They need no rhetoric. They speak for themselves.

"I hope I will live to see the day when, as in the early days of our country, we won't have any public schools. The churches will have taken them over again and Christians will be running them."—Rev. Jerry Falwell (see the section titled In Other Words).

"Secular schools can never be tolerated because such a school has no religious instruction and a general moral instruction without a religious foundation is built on air; consequently, all character training and religion must be derived from faith. . . . We need believing people."—Adolf Hitler, April 26, 1933, speech during negotiations leading to the Nazi-Vatican Concordat

"God wants me to run for president."—George W. Bush, 2000 campaign statement

"I am convinced that I am acting as the agent of our Creator. By fighting off the Jews, I am doing the Lord's work."—Adolf Hitler, *Mein Kampf*

So here we are.

You, me, and this little book—this toolkit—in your hands.

As a writer and a reader, I trust the power of words that try to tell truths. I believe such words can help save us—our country and our scarred, embattled planet. Tom Paine despaired that his words were hopelessly misunderstood, yet they inspired a revolution. Lincoln, on meeting Harriet Beecher Stowe, author of *Uncle Tom's Cabin*, said, "So this is the little lady who started the Civil War."

I want to start no war—of culture or otherwise. Perhaps naively, I still want to end wars. The sole purpose of *Fighting Words* is to reacquaint my countrymen and countrywomen with our secular roots—and to inspire us to honor them.

Happily, there seems to be a growing hunger for histories of early America and for biographies of the Founders who framed the new nation's Constitution. Still (regrettably), too few people plow through four-hundred-page books. We live in an age and culture of sound-bites and factoids. So I researched and compiled *Fighting Words*—which began life as a short piece in *Ms.* magazine—in hopes of bridging the two: feeding the hunger, but with the sound-bite brevity of modern communications. A tool for arguing. Margins to mark and pages to dog-ear. A source to pull from pocket, purse, or knapsack and brandish, saying, "No! Wait! That's not *true*! *Actually*, James Madison said. . . ." A body of evidence. A database for reference when writing letters to newspapers or debating in school. Or just to delight in feeling vindicated, and in recognizing the Founders not as dusty, pompous, old men in powdered wigs, but as the revolutionaries they actually were.

This book is U.S. specific—although I confess it would have been lovely to include bits from the luminous writing of Mary Wollstonecraft, or from "The Necessity of Atheism" by Percy Bysshe Shelley (an essay that got him expelled from Oxford in 1811). I was tempted to add many quotes like Graham Greene's "Heresy is only another word for freedom of thought," or Albert Camus's "Don't wait for the Last Judgment. It takes place every day." But what does insist on inclusion here is the following paragraph by Alexis de Tocqueville, from his great *Democracy in America*, in 1835: "They all attributed the peaceful dominion of religion in their country mainly to the separation of church and state. I do not hesitate to affirm that during my stay in America I did not meet a single individual, of the clergy or the laity, who was not of the same opinion on this point."

Lucky de Tocqueville.

It's time to reclaim our nation and return it to its original "patriotic" values. These constitute our rightful inheritance, and could serve, as well, as our inspiration. The United States of America was—is—a remarkable experiment, as its Founders realized. To this day, the reason the world wants to come here is not really for the plasma TVs, big cars, fast foods, and commercial hype—especially since these dubious enticements are now being exported around the globe. The real reason the world wants to come here is still to be part of the remarkable experiment.

So it's up to us. You and me.

After the first Constitutional Convention, Benjamin Franklin was asked what type of government the Founders had chosen. Franklin replied, "We have given you a republic—if you can keep it."

Can we keep it?

Robin Morgan
May 2006
New York City

1.

The Founders' Own Fighting Words

The Founders certainly were imperfect men. Some were slaveholders. Others, like Paine, wrote anti-slavery pamphlets, while Franklin organized the first anti-slavery societies. Women were not even on their radar screens—despite Abigail Adams's famous warning to her husband John: "If particular care and attention are not paid to the ladies, we are determined to foment a rebellion and will not hold ourselves bound to obey any laws in which we have no voice or representation."

These men, far from being uniformly Christian, were freethinkers, agnostics, atheists, Christians, Freemasons, and Deists (a Deist professes belief in as-yet-unknown powers evinced in the natural, scientifically observed universe). But religious or not, they fought for a secular state and for freedom of belief.

With all their faults, the Founders were, of course,

revolutionaries. Their own words, as well as the founding documents they forged, are still profoundly radical.

THOMAS PAINE

Paine's early pamphlets and other writings greatly influenced the Founders, but were also denounced as "infidel documents." His words were widely read but were also publicly burned, and are still regarded as controversial. Paine alone among the American Revolutionaries has no formal monument in Washington, D.C., and even the American Quakers refused him burial, though he had been raised a Quaker. Paine was a freethinker, vilified and persecuted as an atheist (although John Adams befriended him, and Thomas Jefferson stood by him when no one else would), but he actually termed himself a Deist. In fact, he attacked the excesses of the French Revolution—including opposing atheism—and was imprisoned by France for this position, requiring the aid of John Adams and James Monroe for his rescue. Yet he relentlessly opposed organized churches, reserving particularly vituperative words for Christianity. Following are some samples from his two greatest works, *The Rights of Man* and *The Age of Reason*.

> Toleration is not the opposite of intoleration, but is the counterfeit of it. Both are despotisms. The one assumes to itself the right of withholding liberty of conscience, and the other of granting it. The one is the Pope armed with fire and faggot, and the other is

the Pope selling or granting indulgences.—*The Rights of Man*, 1791

My country is the world and my religion is to do good.—*The Rights of Man*

I do not believe in the creed professed by the Jewish church, by the Roman church, by the Greek church, by the Protestant church, nor by any church that I know of. My own mind is my church. —*The Age of Reason*, 1793

The creator of man is the creator of science, and it is through that medium that man can see God. —*The Age of Reason*

I feel no need for any other faith than my faith in human beings.— *The Age of Reason*

Of all the systems of religion that ever were invented, there is no more derogatory to the Almighty, more unedifying to man, more repugnant to reason, and more contradictory to itself than this thing called Christianity.—*The Age of Reason*

Persecution is not an original feature in any religion; but it is always the strongly marked feature of all religions established by law. . . . All national institutions of churches, whether Jewish, Christian, or Turkish, appear to me no other than human inventions set up to terrify and enslave mankind, and monopolize power and profit. . . . I do not mean by this declaration to condemn those who believe otherwise; they have the same right to their belief as I have to mine. But it is necessary to the happiness of man, that he be mentally faithful to himself. Infidelity does not consist in believing, or in disbelieving; it consists in professing to believe what he does not believe.—*The Age of Reason*

The adulterous connection of church and state, wherever it had taken place, whether Jewish, Christian, or Turkish, had so effectually prohibited, by pains and penalties, every discussion upon established creeds, and upon first principles of religion, that until the system of government should be changed, those subjects could not be brought fairly and openly before the world; but that whenever this should be done, a revolution in the system of religion would follow.—*The Age of Reason*

All this war-whoop of the pulpit has some concealed object. Religion is not the Cause, but it is the stalking horse.—*The Age of Reason*

ETHAN ALLEN

War hero and typical Revolutionary secularist, Allen was as militantly anticlerical as he was antimonarchical, seeing the two as closely connected. His book, *Reason the Only Oracle of Man,* was denounced by Reverend Timothy Dwight, president of Yale and a leader of religious orthodoxy, as "the first formal publication in the United States openly directed against the Christian religion."

Who would imagine that the Deity conducts his providence similar to the detestable despots of the world?

Oh horrible, most horrible impeachment of divine Goodness! —*Reason the Only Oracle of Man*, 1784

While we are under the tyranny of priests . . . it will ever be in their interest, to invalidate the law of nature and reason, in order to establish systems incompatible therewith.—*Reason the Only Oracle of Man*

BENJAMIN FRANKLIN

Franklin, elder statesman of the Founders, was raised a Calvinist, but rebelled early against his parents' adherence to Christianity. Furthermore, he worked lifelong to spread that rebellion, and influenced both Jefferson and Adams in this respect. In fact, Franklin's friend, Dr. Priestley, wrote in his own *Autobiography*: "It is much to be lamented that a man of Franklin's general good character and great influence should have been an unbeliever in Christianity, and also have done as much as he did to make others unbelievers." Franklin, a scientist, called himself a "thorough Deist," rejecting churches, rituals, and "supernatural superstitions." His many *Poor Richard's Almanac* aphorisms have entered daily usage, but tamed, shorn of their original context. For example, his famous advice, "God helps those who help themselves," takes on a sharp tone when understood in the context of his other writings, and especially in the company of the other Founders.

My parents had given me betimes religious impressions, and I received from my infancy a pious education in the principles of Calvinism. But scarcely was I arrived at fifteen years of age, when, after having doubted in turn of different tenets, according as I found them combated in the different books that I read, I began to doubt of Revelation itself.—*Autobiography* (1731–1759)

Some [Christian] books against Deism fell into my hands. . . . It happened that they wrought an effect on me quite contrary to what was intended by them; for the arguments of the Deists, which were quoted to be refuted, appeared to me much stronger than the refutations; in short, I soon became a thorough Deist.— *Autobiography*

If we look back into history for the character of the present sects in Christianity, we shall find few that have not in their turns been persecutors, and complainers of persecution. The primitive Christians thought persecution extremely wrong in the Pagans, but practiced it on one another. The first Protestants of the Church of England blamed persecution in the Romish church, but practiced it upon the Puritans. These found it wrong in the Bishops, but fell into the same practice themselves both here [England] and in New England.—Essay "On Toleration"

When a religion is good, I conceive it will support itself; and when it does not support itself, and God does not take care to support it so that its professors are obliged to call for help of the civil power, 'tis a sign, I apprehend, of its being a bad one.—Letter to Richard Price, October 9, 1790

GEORGE WASHINGTON

The misleading image of Washington as a devout Christian was forged by Mason Locke Weems, who published an influential biography, *The Life of George Washington*, in 1800 (Weems also invented the cherry-tree story). Washington was a Freemason; he became a Master Mason in 1799. (Ben Franklin, Alexander Hamilton, and John Hancock also accepted Freemasonry, since the society was committed to freedom of belief.) After Washington's death, his close friend Dr. Abercrombie confirmed that he had been a Deist. Washington rarely alluded to religion, referred to divinity as "It," and never mentioned the name of Jesus Christ in any of his literally thousands of letters. He was publicly criticized for spending Sundays "in secular pursuits," and when he did (rarely) attend church, he stood during prayers while others knelt, and always left before communion, rather pointedly displaying his disbelief in the central ceremony of Christian faith. Washington's famous deathbed scene at Mount Vernon in 1799 was attended by three doctors and several servants but not one clergyman; in the words of one witness, there was "no word or act which can be turned to the service of superstition, cant, or bigotry." Jefferson wrote in his private journal, February 1800, "I know that Gouverneur Morris, who claimed to be in his secrets, and believed himself to be so, has often told me that General Washington believed no more in that system [Christianity] than he did." But Washington was a

staunch defender of every individual's religious rights—
and of the separation of religion from government. In
May 1789, he wrote to the United Baptist Churches in
Virginia that everyone "ought to be protected in worshipping the Deity according to the dictates of his own
conscience." Washington initiated such documents as
The Treaty of Tripoli, which states, "the Government of
the United States of America is not in any sense
founded on the Christian religion." (See the section
titled The Law.) He firmly espoused a secular nation,
embracing citizens who worshipped different faiths or
those who believed in none.

Among many other weighty objections to the
Measure, it has been suggested, that it [appointing
chaplains] has a tendency to introduce religious dis-
putes into the Army, which above all things should
be avoided, and in many instances would compel
men to a mode of Worship which they do not profess.—Letter to John Hancock, then president of
Congress, expressing opposition to a congressional
plan to appoint brigade chaplains in the Continental
Army (1777)

I am not less ardent in my wish that you may succeed in your plan of toleration in religious matters.
Being no bigot myself, I am disposed to indulge the
professors of Christianity in the church that road to
heaven which to them shall seem the most direct. . . .
—Letter to Lafayette, 1787

Happily, the Government of the United States, which gives to bigotry no sanction, to persecution no assistance, requires only that they who live under its protection should demean themselves as good citizens in giving it on all occasions their effective support.—Letter to the Jewish Congregation of Rhode Island, 1790

Of all the animosities which have existed among mankind, those which are caused by difference of sentiment in religion appear to be the most inveterate and distressing, and ought most to be deprecated.—Letter to Sir Edward Newenham, 1792

JOHN ADAMS

Adams's writings are among those most stirring in defense of a secular state. The Treaty of Tripoli (see George Washington) was passed by Congress during Adams's presidency, and he signed it (see the section titled The Law). Adams was a Unitarian, deeply influenced by the ideas of the Enlightenment. He vociferously opposed doctrines of supernaturalism or of eternal damnation. He also fully realized just how radical these ideas were:

The United States of America have exhibited, perhaps, the first example of governments erected on the simple principles of nature; and if men are now sufficiently enlightened to disabuse themselves of artifice, imposture, hypocrisy, and superstition, they

will consider this event as an era in their history. . . .
It will never be pretended that any persons employed
in that service [forming the U.S. government] had
interviews with the gods, or were in any degree under
the influence of Heaven, more than those at work
upon ships or houses, or laboring in merchandise or
agriculture; it will forever be acknowledged that
these governments were contrived merely by the use
of reason and the senses. Thirteen governments [of
the original states] thus founded on the natural
authority of the people alone, without a pretence of
miracle or mystery . . . are a great point gained in
favor of the rights of mankind.—from *A Defence of
the Constitutions of Government of the United States of
America*, 1787–1788

I almost shudder at the thought of alluding to
the most fatal example of the abuses of grief which
the history of mankind has preserved—the Cross.
Consider what calamities that engine of grief has
produced!—Letter to Thomas Jefferson

THOMAS JEFFERSON

Jefferson, author of the Declaration of Independence
(see the section titled The Genuine Articles: Uncen-
sored), repeatedly attacked religion's practices as superstitions, referring to the clerical establishment as
"cannibal priests." He said and wrote clearly that he did
not believe in the Trinity or in the divinity of Jesus
Christ, although he respected the moral teachings of

whoever might have been an historical Jesus, ranking him with Socrates. He even cut up parts of a copy of the New Testament and reassembled them, to rescue the "pure principles which he [Jesus] taught," from the "artificial vestments in which they have been muffled by priests, who have travestied them into various forms as instruments of riches and power for themselves." (*The Jefferson Bible* is still available in a 1989 reissue from Beacon Press, Boston.) Nor did Jefferson believe in miracles, saints, salvation, damnation, or angelic presences. He strongly opposed those who, like Patrick Henry, wanted to establish some form of theocratic Christian state (for Virginia and, later, for the new nation). In fact, in 1798, Alexander Hamilton—himself a devout Episcopalian who tried to found a Christian Constitutional Society—accused Jefferson and other Founders of "a conspiracy to establish atheism on the ruins of Christianity." When Jefferson founded the University of Virginia, he again provoked attacks denouncing him as an "Infidel," for having insisted that no religious faith should be taught at the University as part of its course of instruction. Jefferson refused to issue proclamations of thanksgiving or prayer during his years in office, noting that "civil powers alone have been given to the President of the United States, and no authority to direct the religious exercises of his constituents." Reason, materialism, and science were Jefferson's strongest influences, as his prolific writings consistently demonstrate:

An amendment was proposed by inserting "Jesus Christ," so that it [the preamble] would read "A departure from the plan of Jesus Christ, the holy author of our religion"; the insertion was rejected by the great majority, in proof that they meant to comprehend, within the mantle of its protection, the Jew and the Gentile, the Christian and Mohammedan, the Hindoo and Infidel of every denomination.— From Jefferson's *Autobiography*, referring to the Virginia Act for Religious Freedom. Jefferson introduced this statute, which became Virginia law in 1779, to frustrate Patrick Henry's attempts to establish "some form of Christian worship" for Virginia, and to ensure an emphatic separation of religion from government. (See also the section titled The Law.)

Is uniformity [of opinion] obtainable? Millions of innocent men, women, and children, since the introduction of Christianity, have been burnt, tortured, fined, and imprisoned; yet we have not advanced one inch towards uniformity. What has been the effect of coercion? To make one half the world fools, and the other half hypocrites.—Notes on the State of Virginia, 1781–1785

It does me no injury for my neighbor to say there are twenty gods or no God. It neither picks my pocket nor breaks my leg.—Notes on the State of Virginia, 1782

No man shall be compelled to frequent or support any religious worship, ministry, or place whatsoever;

nor shall be enforced, restrained, molested, or burdened in his body or goods; nor shall otherwise suffer on account of his religious opinion or belief: but all men shall be free to profess and by argument to maintain their opinions.—Text authored by Jefferson in 1779 for the Statute of Virginia for Religious Freedom, which repealed taxation measures for state-supported churches

Question with boldness even the existence of a god, because if there be one, he must more approve of the homage of reason then that of blindfolded fear.—Letter to Peter Carr, August 10, 1787

I never submitted the whole system of my opinions to the creed of any party of men whatever in religion, in philosophy, in politics, or in anything else where I was capable of thinking for myself. Such an addiction is the last degradation of a free and moral agent.—Letter to Francis Hopkinson, March 13, 1789

They [the clergy] believe that any portion of power confided to me, will be exerted in opposition to their schemes. And they believe rightly; for I have sworn upon the altar of god, eternal hostility against every form of tyranny over the mind of man. But this is all they have to fear from me: and enough, too, in their opinion.—Letter to Dr. Benjamin Rush, September 23, 1800

Sometimes it is said that man cannot be trusted with the government of himself. Can he, then, be trusted with the government of others? Or have we found angels in the forms of kings to govern him? Let history answer this question.—First Inaugural Address, March 4, 1801

Believing with you that religion is a matter which lies solely between man and his god, that he owes account to none other for his faith or his worship, that the legislative powers of government reach actions only, and not opinions, I contemplate with sovereign reverence that act of the whole American people which declared that their legislature should *"make no law respecting an establishment of religion, or prohibiting the free exercise thereof," thus building a wall of separation between church and State.*—Letter to the Danbury [Connecticut] Baptist Association, January 1, 1802

Politics, like religion, hold up the torches of martyrdom to the reformers of error.—Letter to James Oglivie, August 4, 1811

History, I believe, furnishes no example of a priest-ridden people maintaining a free civil government. This marks the lowest grade of ignorance of which their civil as well as religious leaders will always avail themselves for their own purposes.—Letter to Alexander von Humboldt, December 6, 1813

The whole history of these books [the Gospels] is so defective and doubtful that it seems vain to attempt minute enquiry into it: and such tricks have been played with their text, and with the texts of other books relating to them, that we have a right, from that cause, to entertain much doubt what parts of them are genuine. In the New Testament there is internal evidence that parts of it have proceeded from an extraordinary man; and that other parts are of the fabric of very inferior minds. It is as easy to separate those parts, as to pick out diamonds from dunghills.—Letter to John Adams, January 24, 1814

Christianity neither is, nor ever was a part of the common law.—Letter to Dr. Thomas Cooper, February 10, 1814. (See also the section titled The Law.)

In every country and in every age, the priest has been hostile to liberty. He is always in alliance with the despot, abetting his abuses in return for protection to his own.—Letter to Horatio G. Spafford, March 17, 1814

If we did a good act merely from love of God and a belief that it is pleasing to Him, whence arises the morality of the Atheist? . . . Their virtue, then, must have had some other foundation than the love of God.—Letter to Thomas Law, June 13, 1814

You say you are a Calvinist. I am not. I am of a sect by myself, as far as I know.—Letter to Ezra Stiles Ely, June 25, 1819

As you say of yourself, I too am an Epicurian. I consider the genuine (not the imputed) doctrines of Epicurus as containing everything rational in moral philosophy which Greece and Rome have left us. —Letter to William Short, October 31, 1819

Among the sayings and discourses imputed to him [Jesus] by his biographers, I find many passages of fine imagination, correct morality, and of the most lovely benevolence; and others again of so much ignorance, so much absurdity, so much untruth, charlatanism, and imposture, as to pronounce it impossible that such contradictions should have proceeded from the same being.—Letter to William Short, April 13, 1820

To talk of immaterial existences is to talk of nothings. To say that the human soul, angels, god, are immaterial, is to say they are nothings, or that there is no god, no angels, no soul. I cannot reason otherwise: but I believe I am supported in my creed of materialism by Locke, Tracy, and Stewart.—Letter to John Adams, August 15, 1820

And the day will come when the mystical generation of Jesus, by the supreme being as his father in the womb of a virgin, will be classed with the fable of the generation of Minerve in the brain of Jupiter. — Letter to John Adams, April 11, 1823

It is between fifty and sixty years since I read it [the Apocalypse], and I then considered it merely the ravings of a maniac, no more worthy nor capable of explanation than the incoherences of our own nightly dreams.—Letter to General Alexander Smyth, January 17, 1825

I know also that laws and institutions must go hand in hand with the progress of the human mind. As that becomes more developed, more enlightened, as new discoveries are made, new truths disclosed, and manners and opinions change with the change of circumstances, institutions must advance also, and keep pace with the times. We might as well require a man to wear still the same coat which fitted him when a boy, as civilized society to remain ever under the regimen of their barbarous ancestors.—To Samuel Kercheval, July 12, 1810, and inscribed at the Jefferson Memorial in Washington, D.C.

JAMES MADISON

Madison, "the father of the Constitution," opposed all use of "religion as an engine of civil policy." Devout in his youth, he retained a more moderate faith as he matured, yet consistently delivered passionate warnings about religion's role in the state—for the protection of both. He chaired the House conference committee on the Bill of Rights, and the wording in his own draft of the First Amendment, delivered in a speech in the House of Representatives, 1789, was both more specific and more inclusive than the final version: *"the civil rights of none shall be abridged on account of religious belief or worship, nor shall any national religion be established, nor shall the full and equal rights of conscience be in any manner, or on any pretext, infringed."* Madison also accurately prophesied the threat of "ecclesiastical corporations," and even opposed the idea of chaplains for Congress and for the armed forces:

Religious bondage shackles and debilitates the mind and unfits it for every noble enterprize, every expanded prospect.—Letter to William Bradford, April 1, 1774

During almost fifteen centuries has the legal establishment of Christianity been on trial. What have been its fruits? More or less in all places, pride and indolence in the Clergy, ignorance and servility in the laity; in both, superstition, bigotry and persecution. — *Memorial and Remonstrance against Religious Assessments*, 1785, Section 7

What influence, in fact, have ecclesiastical establishments had on society? In some instances they have been seen to erect a spiritual tyranny on the ruins of the civil authority; on many instances they have been seen upholding the thrones of political tyranny; in no instance have they been the guardians of the liberties of the people. Rulers who wish to subvert the public liberty may have found an established clergy convenient auxiliaries. A just government, instituted to secure and perpetuate it, needs them not.—*Memorial and Remonstrance against Religious Assessments*

The free men of America did not wait till usurped power had strengthened itself by exercise, and entangled the question in precedents. They saw all the consequences in the principle, and they avoided the consequences by denying the principle. We revere this lesson too much soon to forget it.

Who does not see that the same authority which can establish Christianity, in exclusion of all other Religions, may establish with the same ease any particular sect of Christians, in exclusion of all other Sects? . . . Distant as it may be in its present form from the Inquisition, it differs from it only in degree. The one is the first step, the other the last in the career of intolerance.—*Memorial and Remonstrance Against Religious Assessments*

The danger of silent accumulations & encroachments by Ecclesiastical Bodies have not sufficiently engaged attention in the United States. . . . But besides the danger of a direct mixture of Religion & Civil Government, there is an evil which ought to be guarded against in the indefinite accumulation of property from the capacity of holding it in perpetuity by ecclesiastical corporations. The power of all corporations ought to be limited in this respect. The growing wealth acquired by them never fails to be a source of abuses.—From a Detached Memoranda, also titled "Monopolies, Perpetuities, Corporations, Ecclesiastical Endowments," ca. 1817

Is the appointment of Chaplains to the two Houses of Congress consistent with the Constitution, and with the pure principle of religious freedom? In strictness the answer on both points must be in the negative. . . . *The establishment of the chaplainship to Congress is a palpable violation of equal rights, as well as of Constitutional principles. . . .* Better also to disarm, in the same way, the precedent of Chaplainships for the army and navy, than erect them into a political authority in matters of religion. —From a Detached Memoranda, also titled "Monopolies, Perpetuities, Corporations, Ecclesiastical Endowments"

Religious proclamations by the Executive [branch] recommending thanksgivings & fasts are shoots from the same root with the legislative acts [above] reviewed. Altho' recommendations only, they imply a religious agency, making no part of the trust delegated to political rulers. . . . [such acts] seem to imply and certainly nourish the erroneous idea of a national religion . . . a theocracy having been improperly adopted by so many nations which have embraced Christianity, is too apt to lurk in the bosoms even of Americans, who in general are aware of the distinction between religious and political societies. . . . The last and not the least objection is the liability of the practice to subserviency to political views; to the scandal of religion, as well as the increase of party animosities. Candid or incautious politicians will not always disown such views.—From a Detached Memoranda, also titled "Monopolies, Perpetuities, Corporations, Ecclesiastical Endowments"

And I have no doubt that every new example will succeed, as every past one has done, in shewing that religion & Govt will both exist in greater purity, the less they are mixed together.—Letter to Edward Livingston, July 10, 1822

The finiteness of the human understanding betrays itself on all subjects but more especially when it contemplates such as involve infinity . . . the mind at once prefers the idea of a self-existing cause to that of an infinite series of cause and effect . . . and it finds more facility in assenting to the self-existence of an invisible cause, possessing infinite power, wisdom, and goodness, than to the self-existence of the Universe, visibly destitute of those attributes, and which may be the effect of them. In this comparative facility of conception and belief, all philosophical reasoning on the subject must, perhaps, terminate. —Letter to Reverend F. Beasley, 1825

2.

The Genuine Articles: Uncensored

THE DECLARATION OF INDEPENDENCE
Religionists often quote the Declaration as if it were a document of governance. It is not. The Constitution and the Bill of Rights are the U.S. documents of governance. The Declaration had just one purpose: to dissolve the political ties with England. Consequently, it specified grievances about laws, taxation, representation, and so on—but *not one word about religion*.

It is a document reflective of its time, sometimes sadly so (e.g., the mention of "merciless Savages," the invisibility of female citizens, all lack of reference to slavery, and the use of "man" and "mankind" as generic terms for "people" and "humanity"). But it is a document also heavily influenced by the ideas of the Enlightenment, and one deliberately striving to leap ahead of its time, inspiring its people to rise to a new vision.

The Founders were radicals. They based the authority of the Declaration on the then-shocking concept that governments were instituted among ordinary people, and thus derived their just powers from the consent of the governed. This directly challenged the European traditions of rule by divine right and/or heavenly authority. We should never forget: George III was not only king of England but also the anointed head of its church.

Thomas Jefferson, who drafted the Declaration, vocally opposed orthodoxy in all forms. He regarded Christianity as yet another superstition, and rejected any notion of supernatural beings. (See the section titled The Founders' Own Fighting Words.)

In his original draft of the Declaration, the word "Creator" was notably absent. The original draft read:

> We hold these truths to be sacred and undeniable, that all men are created equal and independent; that from that equal creation they derive in rights inherent and unalienables, among which are the preservation of life, and liberty and the pursuit of happiness.

Under pressure, Jefferson revised the text to the now-familiar:

> We hold these Truths to be self-evident, that all Men are created equal, that they are endowed by their Creator with certain unalienable Rights, that among these are Life, Liberty and the Pursuit of Happiness.

In the first paragraph of the document, the words "to which the Laws of Nature and of Nature's God entitle them" do appear. But *in the context* of a time (and author) so intensely influenced by the Enlightenment and by science, "Nature's God" and "Divine Providence" are analogous to such contemporary phrases as "powers to date beyond our understanding," "nature," "the life force," or even "a unified field theory"; indeed, Washington referred to Deity as "it."

The Declaration purposefully makes *no* reference to the Judeo-Christian tradition, Christianity, or any organized religion whatsoever. It's the Genuine Article.

For the full text, see the section titled After Words.

THE CONSTITUTION

The Constitution contains not one reference to a deity or to any supernatural powers.

This is not an oversight.

On the contrary, the word "religious" arises only once:

Article VI: The Senators and Representatives before mentioned, and the members of the several state legislatures, and all executive and judicial officers, both of the United States and of the several states, shall be bound by oath or affirmation, to support this Constitution; but no religious test shall ever be required as a qualification to any office or public trust under the United States.

That a secular choice of *"affirmation"* is listed as the coequal alternative to a religious *"oath"* is, in itself, astonishing for its time; to insist on affirming rather than swearing is still controversial, although totally legal, today. The Framers of the 1787 document that founded and governs the United States were passionately opposed to any merging of church and state—not only because it would prove oppressive to the freedom to worship (or *not* to worship) as one chose, but also because they knew well that such merging would prove oppressive to the secular freedoms of citizens of the state and to the integrity of the state itself.

James Madison, the "father of the Constitution," was a radical defender of the separation of church and state. (See The Founders; also see After Words for the full texts of The Constitution, The Bill of Rights, and the other Amendments.)

THE BILL OF RIGHTS: AMENDMENTS 1-10 AND LATER AMENDMENTS TO THE CONSTITUTION

Passed in 1789, less than two years after the Constitution, the first ten Amendments are focused on individual rights and liberties—again, a radical concept for the time.

Most people today think of the First Amendment as ensuring "freedom of speech." Actually, "Congress shall make no law respecting an establishment of religion, or prohibiting the free exercise thereof" *are the first words of the First Amendment.* The Founders apparently considered a secular government plus religious freedom so crucial that they list these—with the Establishment Clause *first*—even *before* the freedoms of speech, the press, assembly, and so on (see The Law; also see After Words for the full text of the Bill of Rights and the later Amendments).

THE PRESIDENTIAL OATH OF OFFICE

The only vow of office specified verbatim in the Constitution is the one taken by the president. *It makes absolutely no mention of a deity, and the words "so help me God" do not appear in it.* On the contrary, the Founders deliberately noted that the vow could be sworn as an oath or simply *affirmed*—a radical notion for the time.

> ARTICLE II, SECTION 1 OF THE CONSTITUTION
> Before he enter on the execution of his office, he shall take the following oath or affirmation: "I do solemnly swear (or affirm) that I will faithfully execute the office of President of the United States, and will to the best of my ability, preserve, protect and defend the Constitution of the United States."

That's the whole of it. Period.

THE PLEDGE OF ALLEGIANCE

"Traditionalists" are rabid to keep inserting "under God" in the Pledge of Allegiance. But they are actually *anti*tradition.

Those two words never appeared in the original pledge, penned in 1892 by Francis Bellamy (a Baptist minister forced to resign the pulpit for having called himself a Christian socialist). After lengthy, intense lobbying by the Knights of Columbus and the American Legion, "One nation, indivisible" was changed by Congress to "One nation *under God*, indivisible"; this was as late as 1954, reflecting McCarthyite bombast against "godless Communism" at the height of the Cold War. (Francis Bellamy's granddaughter, Barbara Bellamy Wright, has denounced the insertion, claiming that her grandfather "would have objected strongly to this change, as it changed the fundamental meaning . . . he had considered that 'one nation, indivisible' conveyed the deep meaning that after the Civil War our nation could not be divided.")

On Flag Day in 1943, the U.S. Supreme Court (in *West Virginia State Board of Education v. Barnette*) ruled unconstitutional a law compelling schoolchildren to recite the Pledge and salute the flag. Writing for the Court, Justice Robert H. Jackson declared, "If there is any fixed star in our constitutional constellation, it is that no official, high or petty, can prescribe what shall be orthodox in politics, nationalism, religion, or other matters of opinion."

THE [ORIGINAL] PLEDGE OF ALLEGIANCE
I pledge allegiance to the flag of the United States of America, and to the Republic for which it stands. One nation, indivisible, with liberty and justice for all.

COIN OF THE REALM

Originally, the motto on U.S. coins (the major exchange medium in the eighteenth century) was simply the word "Liberty."

"In God We Trust" began to appear informally on some U.S. coins during the nineteenth century, due to a spread of religious intensity following the agonies of the Civil War. But when, early in the twentieth century, President Theodore Roosevelt commissioned the design for new coinage, he made a point of leaving the words *off*, expressing his "very firm conviction that to put such a motto ["in God We Trust"] on coins . . . not only does no good but does positive harm." Yet Congress overrode him, formally legislating the four words for coins in 1908—this, after a lengthy crusade initiated by a hyper-religious director of the Mint, James Pollock. A well-organized outcry, including petitions from religious congregations, frightened Rough Rider Roosevelt so much that he conceded, announcing that he would not veto the bill.

Despite having slowly become the principal medium of exchange during the following decades, paper currency escaped being "godded up" until 1957. Religious advocates began agitating for the words on paper currency during the 1940s, in the wake of World War II, but not until the more welcoming political climate of the 1950s did they succeed. The 1950s also saw IGWT's adoption as the national "motto," now ensconced on a wall in the U.S. House of Representatives.

The Founders would be outraged. Their original "motto" and Great Seal—devised by John Adams, Benjamin Franklin, and Thomas Jefferson—was "E Pluribus Unum" ("From Many, One."), which, with "Liberty," was considered sufficient and appropriate until the charge of the god brigades. (See the section titled The Founders' Own Fighting Words.)

3.

(More) U.S. Presidents' Fighting Words

Maintaining the strict separation of church and state intended by the Founders has never been easy or assured. Below is a sampling of quotes from various American presidents—Democratic, Republican, and even Whig—who defended this concept, as enshrined in the Constitution, against repeated waves of assault by what James Madison termed "ecclesiastical establishments" and religious revivalists.

JOHN QUINCY ADAMS

The question about keeping the Sabbath holy as a day of rest is one of the numerous religious and political excitements which keep the free people of this Union in perpetual agitation. . . . There are in this country, as in all others, a certain proportion of restless and turbulent spirits—poor, unoccupied, ambitious—who must always have something to quarrel about with their neighbors. These people are the authors of religious revivals.—Entry in personal diary, January 21, 1844

ANDREW JACKSON

Whilst I concur with the synod in the efficacy of prayer and in the hope that our country may be preserved from the attack of pestilence . . . I am constrained to decline the appointment of any period or mode as proper for the public manifestation of this reliance. I could not do otherwise without transcending those limits which are prescribed by the Constitution for the President, and without feeling that I might in some degree disturb the security which religion now enjoys in this country in its complete separation from the political concerns of the General Government.—Reply to the Reformed Church and other religious groups and legislators urging him to declare a national day of fasting and prayer to combat a cholera epidemic in eastern North America

ZACHARY TAYLOR

I have yet thought it most proper to leave the subject of a Thanksgiving Proclamation where custom in many parts of the country has so long consigned it, in the hands of the Governors of the several States.—Letter to Reverend Nicholas Murray, 1849, refusing to issue a federal proclamation

MILLARD FILLMORE

I am tolerant of all creeds. Yet if any sect suffered itself to be used for political objects I would meet it by political opposition. In my view church and state should be separate, not only in form, but fact. Religion and politics should not be mingled.—Speech during the 1856 presidential election

ABRAHAM LINCOLN

Lincoln has led scholars a merry chase regarding his stand on religion, so that both religionists and secularists claim him as their own. In his youth, Lincoln seems to have been intensely anti-Christian. His first law partner, John T. Stuart, noted, "he was an avowed and open infidel, and sometimes bordered on Atheism. He went further against Christian beliefs and doctrines and principles than any man I ever heard." Later, although Lincoln seems to have become a believer in "fate," he was never baptized or joined a church, rejecting organized religion in much the same way as the Founders had. Still, he was a canny, ambitious politician capable of bending when forced to, and some of his public pronouncements reflect that. He burned an early manuscript he had written—arguing against divine authorship of or inspiration for the Bible—after his friend Samuel Hill warned him that its publication would have disastrous effects on his getting elected. On separation of church and state Lincoln was clear, stating, "*The United States government must not undertake to run the churches.* When an individual, in the church or out of it, becomes dangerous to the public interest, he must be checked." Interestingly, *Lincoln's own first draft of the Emancipation Proclamation makes no mention of any deity*, but he responded to pressure and added the words "the gracious favor of Almighty God." Similarly, *the words "under God" do not appear in either his first or second drafts of the Gettysburg Address*. We can also discern Lincoln's intent from his words about adherence to the Founders' intentions in his anti-slavery Cooper Union speech (see below) regarding the Constitution.

Friends, I agree with you in Providence; but I believe in the Providence of the most men, the largest purse, and the longest cannon.—Speech in Kansas, 1856

All the powers of the earth seem rapidly combining against him [the Negro]. Mammon is after him . . . and the theology of the day is fast joining in the cry. —Lincoln Memorial Album

It will not do to investigate the subject of religion too closely, as it will lead to Infidelity.—Quoted in an interview in *Manfred's Magazine*

What is the frame of government under which we live? The answer must be: "The Constitution of the United States." I fully endorse this. . . . But you say you are conservative—eminently conservative—while we [abolitionists] are revolutionary, destructive, or something of the sort. What is conservatism? Is it not adherence to the old and tried, against the new and untried? We stick to the identical old policy . . . adopted by "our fathers who framed the Government under which we live"; while you with one accord reject, and scout, and spit upon that old policy, and insist upon substituting something new. . . . I do not mean to say we are bound to follow implicitly in whatever our fathers did. To do so, would be to discard all the lights of current experience—to reject all progress— all improvement. What I do say is, that if we would supplant the opinions and policy of our fathers in any case, we should do so upon evidence so conclusive, and argument so clear, that even their great authority, fairly considered and weighed, cannot stand; and most surely not in a case whereof we ourselves declare they understood the question better than we. . . . Let us have faith that right makes might, and in that faith, let us, to the end, dare to do our duty as we understand it.—The famous "Cooper Union Speech" against slavery, which cemented Lincoln's national reputation as abolitionist and charismatic political figure: *In Vindication of the Policy of the Framers of the Constitution*: The Cooper Institute, February 1860

I hope it will not be irreverent for me to say that if it is probable that God would reveal his will to others . . . it might be supposed he would reveal it directly to me. . . . These are not, however, the days of miracles. . . . I must study the plain, physical facts of the case, ascertain what is possible, and learn what appears to be wise and right.—Statement to Chicago Christian ministers, 1863, in *The Collected Works of Abraham Lincoln*, vol. 5 (New Brunswick: Rutgers University Press, 1953)

Both [sides in the Civil War] read the same Bible, and

pray to the same God; and each invokes his aid against
the other. It may seem strange that any men should dare
to ask a just God's assistance in wringing their bread from
the sweat of other men's faces; but let us judge not that we
be not judged.—Second inaugural address, 1865

ULYSSES S. GRANT

No political party can, or ought to, exist when one of its
cornerstones is opposition to freedom of thought. If a sect
sets up its laws as binding above the State laws, whenever
the two come in conflict, this claim must be resisted and
suppressed at all costs.—*Memoirs*, Vol. I, 1885

Leave the matter of religion to the family altar, the
church, and the private schools supported entirely by private contributions. Keep the church and state forever
separate.—Speech to the army of the Tennessee, delivered in Iowa, 1875

JAMES A. GARFIELD

The divorce between Church and State ought to be
absolute. It ought to be so absolute that no church property, anywhere, in any state, or in the nation, should be
exempt from equal taxation; for if you exempt the property of any Church organization, to that extent you
impose a tax upon the whole community.—Speech to
Congress, 1874 (although himself a devout Christian
who had been a preacher in his youth)

THEODORE ROOSEVELT

To discriminate against a thoroughly upright citizen because he belongs to some particular church, or because, like Abraham Lincoln, he has not avowed his allegiance to any church, is an outrage against that liberty of conscience which is one of the foundations of American life.—Theodore Roosevelt, letter to J. C. Martin, November 9, 1908

I hold that in this country there must be complete severance of Church and State; that public moneys shall not be used for the purpose of advancing any particular creed; and therefore that the public schools shall be nonsectarian and no public moneys appropriated for sectarian schools.—Speech at Carnegie Hall, October 12, 1915

(See also subsection titled Coin of the Realm.)

WILLIAM HOWARD TAFT

There is nothing so despicable as a secret society that is based upon religious prejudice and that will attempt to defeat a man because of his religious beliefs. Such a society is like a cockroach—it thrives in the dark. So do those who combine for such an end.—Speech, December 20, 1914

WOODROW WILSON

Of course, like every other man of education and intelligence, I do believe in organic Evolution. It surprises me that at this late date such questions should be raised.—Letter to Professor Curtis written while president, 1922

CALVIN COOLIDGE

The fundamental precept of liberty is toleration. We cannot permit any inquisition either from within or from without the law or apply any religious test to the holding of office. The mind of America must be forever free.—Inaugural Address, 1925

FRANKLIN DELANO ROOSEVELT

The lessons of religious toleration—a toleration which recognizes complete liberty of human thought, liberty of conscience—is one which, by precept and example, must be inculcated in the hearts and minds of all Americans if the institutions of our democracy are to be maintained and perpetuated.—Letter to the Calvert Associates, 1937

HARRY S. TRUMAN

Not all of Jefferson's ideas were popular, though most of them were absolutely right. . . . He was also called an atheist because he didn't believe in a state church, an official church of the government, and in fact made it clear that he didn't much like any church at all . . . it was Jefferson, as governor of Virginia, who wrote the Statute of Religious Liberty in 1786, which said that "no man shall be compelled to frequent or support any religious worship."—*Where the Buck Stops; The Personal and Private Writings of Harry S. Truman,* ed. by Margaret Truman (New York: Warner Books, Inc., 1989)

JOHN F. KENNEDY

I believe in an America where the separation of church and state is absolute—where no Catholic prelate would tell the President (should he be Catholic) how to act, and no Protestant minister would tell his parishioners for whom to vote—where no church or church school is granted any public funds or political preference—and where no man is denied public office merely because his religion differs from the President who might appoint him or the people who might elect him.—Speech to the Greater Houston Ministerial Association, 1960

LYNDON B. JOHNSON

I believe in the American tradition of separation of church and state which is expressed in the First Amendment to the Constitution. By my office—and by personal conviction—I am sworn to uphold that tradition. —Interview, *Baptist Standard,* October, 1964

GERALD R. FORD

It is difficult for me to see how religious exercises can be a requirement in public schools, given our Constitutional requirement of separation of church and state. I feel that the highly desirable goal of religious education must be principally the responsibility of church and home. I do not believe that public education should show any hostility toward religion, and neither should it inhibit voluntary participation, if it does not interfere with the educational process.—Interview, *Los Angeles Herald-Examiner*, October 9, 1976

JIMMY CARTER

I think the government ought to stay out of the religious business.—Quoted in *New York Times*, April 8, 1979

I believe in the separation of church and state and would not use my authority to violate this principle in any way.—Letter to Jack V. Harwell, August 11, 1977

GEORGE HERBERT WALKER BUSH

But the underlying point is, certainly any president of the United States must be always concerned that nothing he or she might do should blur this line of separation between church and state. It is very, very fundamental to our system.—Remarks and a question-and-answer session at the B'nai B'rith International Convention, September 1992

WILLIAM JEFFERSON CLINTON

One thing is indisputable: the First Amendment has protected our freedom to be religious or not religious, as we choose—with the consequence that in this highly secular age the United States is clearly the most conventionally religious country in the entire world, at least the entire industrialized world.—Speech on religious liberty in America at James Madison High School in Vienna, Virginia, 1995

4.

The Law

THE MYTH THAT U.S. LAW IS BASED ON THE TEN COMMANDMENTS

Political religionists often claim that U.S. laws are all "based on" the Ten Commandments. This is patently untrue. Let's leave aside for the moment the fact that there are numerous differing "editions"—including discrepancies between those in Exodus and in Deuteronomy, plus distinct Hebrew, Catholic, and Protestant versions—of what are inaccurately termed the "Ten Commandments." The correct name is "the Decalogue," reflecting what they were called in Biblical Hebrew, Rabbinical Hebrew, and Greek, meaning simply the "Ten Words" or the "Ten Statements." Still, by any name, the Decalogue intersects with U.S. law on only three issues: murder, theft, and perjury. Furthermore, all these crimes had *already* been forbidden in records of civilizations far more ancient than any Judeo-Christian cultures.

In fact, no less a Founder than the author of the Declaration of Independence himself, Thomas Jefferson, directly engaged this false claim about the basis for U.S. law, when he outlined the history of common law in a letter to Thomas Cooper on February 10, 1814:

> For we know that the common law is that system of law which was introduced by the Saxons on their settlement in England, and altered from time to time by proper legislative authority from that time to the date of Magna Charta, which terminates the period of the common law. . . . This settlement took place about the middle of the fifth century. But Christianity was not introduced till the seventh century; the conversion of the first Christian king of the Heptarchy having taken place about the year 598, and that of the last about 686. Here then, was a space of two hundred years, during which the common law was in existence, and Christianity no part of it. . . . [There] were so far alterations of the common law, [which] became themselves a part of it. But none of these adopt Christianity as a part of the common law. If, therefore, from the settlement of the Saxons to the introduction of Christianity among them, that system of religion could not be a part of the common law, because they were not yet Christians, and if, having their laws from that period to the close of the

common law, we are all able to find among them no such act of adoption, we may safely affirm (though contradicted by all the judges and writers on earth) that Christianity neither is, nor ever was a part of the common law.

In that letter to Cooper, Jefferson also summarized how the mistake about Christianity and common law had come about and then proliferated. Jefferson, ever the scholar, found that a *mistranslation* of a Latin term by Prisot, "ancien scripture," had occurred in reference to common-law history. The term meant "ancient scripture" or "older writings" on law—but had incorrectly been interpreted, translated, and then spread as "*Holy* Scripture." Jefferson continued:

And Blackstone repeats [this error in translation], in the words of Sir Matthew Hale, that "Christianity is part of the laws of England," citing Ventris and Strange ubi surpa. 4. Blackst. 59. Lord Mansfield qualifies it a little by saying that "The essential principles of revealed religion are part of the common law" in the case of the *Chamberlain of London v. Evans*, 1767. But he cites no authority, and leaves us at our peril to find out what, in the opinion of the judge, and according to the measure of his foot or his faith, are those essential principles of revealed religion obligatory on us as a part of the common law.

In 2003, the U.S. Supreme Court—having already ruled it unconstitutional to post the Decalogue in public schools *(Stone v. Graham,* 449 U.S. 39, 1980)–refused to review an Alabama State Supreme Court verdict against displaying the Decalogue in a public courthouse. In 2005, two Supreme Court votes set the scene for further confusion and legal battles. A majority voted against a display of the Ten Commandments inside two Kentucky courthouses; joined by John Paul Stevens, Sandra Day O'Connor, Ruth Bader Ginsburg, and Stephen G. Breyer, David Souter wrote, "The touchstone of our analysis is the principle that the First Amendment mandates governmental neutrality between religion and religion, *and between religion and nonreligion"* (italics mine), while Antonin Scalia issued a shocking thirty-page dissent, dismissing the rights of "nonmonotheists" and atheists (see the section titled In *Other* Words). But then a plurality of the court approved a six-foot-tall Decalogue display at the seat of state government. Nevertheless, *Stone* does at least still stand as law (for now): "The preeminent purpose for posting the Ten Commandments on schoolroom walls is plainly religious in nature. . . . The Commandments do not confine themselves to arguably secular matters . . . rather, the first part of the Commandments concerns the *religious* duties of believers: worshipping the Lord God alone, avoiding idolatry, not using the Lord's name in vain, and observing the sabbath day."

THE TREATY OF TRIPOLI

The crucial importance of this Treaty becomes clear when we revisit Article VI, Section II, of the United States Constitution, which reads sternly: "This Constitution, and the Laws of the United States which shall be made in Pursuance thereof; and *all Treaties made, or which shall be made, under the Authority of the United States, shall be the supreme Law of the Land;* and the Judges in every State shall be bound thereby, any Thing in the Constitution or Laws of any State to the Contrary notwithstanding."

The Treaty of Tripoli, initiated by George Washington during his presidency and later signed into law by John Adams on May 26, 1797, during *his* presidency, was/is "a treaty of perpetual peace and friendship between the United States of America and the Bey and subjects of Tripoli, of Barbary."

Here is the full text of a central article of that Treaty, complete with eighteenth-century spellings of the words "Muslims" and "Mohammedan":

ARTICLE 11.

As *the government of the United States of America is not in any sense founded on the Christian Religion,* as it has in itself no character of enmity against the laws, religion or tranquility of Musselmen, and as the said States never have entered into any war or act of hostility against any Mehomitan nation, it is declared by the parties that no pretext arising from religious opinions shall ever produce an interruption of the harmony existing between the two countries.

On June 10, 1797, a few days after having signed the Treaty, Adams issued the following *Proclamation confirming Ratification*, which text was carried in full by major newspapers of the day: "Now be it known, That I, John Adams, President of the United States of America, having seen and considered the said Treaty do, by and with the advice consent of the Senate, accept, ratify, and confirm the same, and every clause and article thereof. And to the End that the said Treaty may be observed and performed with good Faith on the part of the United States, I have ordered the premises to be made public; And I do hereby enjoin and require all persons bearing office civil or military within the United States, and all others citizens or inhabitants thereof, faithfully to observe and fulfil the said Treaty and every clause and article thereof."

THE THREE TESTS

Three tests have evolved from various Supreme Court decisions over time, to decide the constitutionality of laws that have a religious component. These are the three:

1. *The Lemon Test*
[*Lemon v. Kurtzman*, 1971]

(i) a statute [or public policy] must have a secular legislative purpose

(ii) the principal effect of the statute [or policy] must neither advance nor inhibit religion

(iii) the statute [or policy] must not foster "excessive [government] entanglement with religion.

2. *The Endorsement Test*
[*Lynch v. Donnelly,* 1984]

Justice Sandra Day O'Connor first framed the doctrine that if a law favors one religion over another in a manner that makes some people feel like outsiders and others feel like insiders, that law is unconstitutional. Later, after lower courts took her ruling to mean that the phrase "under God" in the Pledge of Allegiance unconstitutionally endorses monotheism, she backpedaled. In a decision voiding the lower court finding, O'Connor then framed this new, four-part "subtest" to govern "ceremonial deism": such acts as the Pledge are constitutional if they: (1) are historical and ubiquitous, (2) are not worship or prayerful, (3) do not refer to a particular religion, and (4) involve minimal religious content.

3. *The Coercion Test*
(*Lee v. Weisman,* 1992)

First enunciated by Justice Anthony Kennedy in a graduation-ceremony-prayer case, this so-called "psychological coercion" standard holds that a law is constitutional, even if it recognizes or accommodates a religion, so long as its demonstration of support does not appear to coerce individuals to support or participate in a religion or religious exercises.

SUPREME COURT JUSTICES' FIGHTING WORDS: A SAMPLING OVER DECADES

JUSTICE ROBERT H. JACKSON

If there is any fixed star in our Constitutional constellation, it is that no official, high or petty, can prescribe what shall be orthodox in politics, nationalism, religion, or other matters of opinion, or force citizens to confess by word or act their faith therein.—*Minersville School District v. Gobitis*, 1940

The day that this country ceases to be free for irreligion, it will cease to be free for religion.—Dissenting opinion, *Zorach v. Clauson*, 1952

JUSTICE HUGO BLACK

The "establishment of religion" clause of the First Amendment means at least this: Neither a state nor the Federal Government can set up a church. Neither can pass laws which aid one religion, aid all religions, or prefer one religion over another. Neither can force nor influence a person to go to or to remain away from church against his will or force him to profess a belief or disbelief in any religion. No person can be punished for entertaining or professing religious beliefs or disbeliefs, for church attendance or nonattendance. No tax in any amount, large or small, can be levied to support any religious activities or institutions, whatever they may be called, or whatever form they may adopt to teach or practice religion. Neither a state nor the Federal Government can, openly or secretly, participate in the affairs of any religious organizations or groups or vice versa. In the words of Jefferson, the clause against establishment of religion by law was intended to erect "a wall of separation between church and state."—Opinion for the Court, *Everson v. Board of Education*, 1947

[I]t is no part of the business of government to compose official prayers for any group of the American people to recite as a part of a religious program carried on by government. It is a matter of history that this very practice of establishing governmentally composed prayers for religious services was one of the reasons which caused many of our early colonists to leave England and seek religious freedom in America.—Opinion for the Court, *Engel v. Vitale*, 1962

JUSTICE FELIX FRANKFURTER

We find that the basic Constitutional principle of absolute separation was violated when the State of Illinois, speaking through its Supreme Court, sustained the school authorities of Champaign in sponsoring and effectively furthering religious beliefs by its educational arrangement. Separation means separation, not something less. Jefferson's metaphor in describing the relation between church and state speaks of a "wall of separation," not of a fine line easily overstepped. The public school is at once the symbol of our democracy and the most pervasive means for promoting our common destiny. In no activity of the state is it more vital to keep out divisive forces than in its schools, to avoid confusing, not to say fusing, what the Constitution sought to keep strictly apart. "The great American principle of eternal separation"—Elihu Root's phrase bears repetition—is one of the vital reliances of our Constitutional system for assuring unities among our people stronger than our diversities. It is the Court's duty to enforce this principle in its full integrity. We renew our conviction that "we have staked the very existence of our country on the faith that complete separation between the state and religion is best for the state and best for religion."—*McCollum v. Board of Education*, 1948

JUSTICE TOM C. CLARK

Finally, we cannot accept that the concept of neutrality, which does not permit a State to require a religious exercise even with the consent of the majority of those affected, collides with the majority's right to free exercise of religion. While the Free Exercise Clause clearly prohibits the use of state action to deny the rights of free exercise to anyone, it has never meant that a majority could use the machinery of the State to practice its beliefs. Such a contention was effectively answered by Mr. Justice Jackson for the Court in *West Virginia Board of Education v. Barnette*: "The very purpose of a Bill of Rights was to withdraw certain subjects from the vicissitudes of political controversy, to place them beyond the reach of majorities and officials and to establish them as legal principles to be applied by the courts. One's right to . . . freedom of worship . . . and other fundamental rights may not be submitted to vote; they depend on the outcome of no elections."—Majority opinion, *School District of Abington Township v. Schempp*, 1963

CHIEF JUSTICE WARREN BURGER

A certain momentum develops in constitutional theory and it can be a "downhill thrust" easily set in motion but difficult to retard or stop. . . . The dangers are increased by the difficulty of perceiving in advance exactly where the "verge" of the precipice lies. As well as constituting an independent evil against which the Religion Clauses were intended to protect, involvement or entanglement between government and religion serves as a warning signal.—*Lemon v. Kurtzman*, 1971

JUSTICE JOHN PAUL STEVENS

The government must pursue a course of complete neutrality toward religion.—Majority opinion, *Wallace v. Jaffree*, 1985

JUSTICE SANDRA DAY O'CONNOR

[G]overnment endorsement . . . of religion . . . sends a message to nonadherents that they are outsiders, not full members of the political community, and an accompanying message to adherents that they are insiders, favored members of the political community.—*Lynch v. Donnelly*, 1984

Those who would renegotiate the boundaries between church and state must therefore answer a difficult question: why would we trade a system that has served us so well for one that has served others so poorly?—*McCreary County Ky. v. ACLU of Kentucky* ("the Ten Commandments ruling"), June 27, 2005

JUSTICE HARRY A. BLACKMUN

Precisely because of the religious diversity that is our national heritage, the Founders added to the Constitution a Bill of Rights, the very first words of which declare: "Congress shall make no law respecting an establishment of religion, or prohibiting the free exercise thereof. . . ." Perhaps in the early days of the Republic these words were understood to protect only the diversity within Christianity, but today they are recognized as guaranteeing religious liberty and equality to "the infidel, the atheist, or the adherent of a non-Christian faith such as Islam or Judaism" (*Wallace v. Jaffre, 1985*).

It is settled law that no government official in this Nation may violate these fundamental constitutional rights regarding matters of conscience.—Decision in *Co. of Allegheny v. ACLU Greater Pittsburgh Chapter* 492 U.S. 573, 1989 (that a manger-creche cannot be raised in front of a county courthouse)

When the government puts its imprimatur on a particular religion it conveys a message of exclusion to all those who do not adhere to the favored beliefs. A government cannot be premised on the belief that all persons are created equal when it asserts that God prefers some.—*Lee v. Weisman,* 1992

JUSTICE ANTHONY KENNEDY
A state-created orthodoxy puts at grave risk that freedom of belief and conscience which are the sole assurance that religious faith is real, not imposed.—Opinion for the Court, *Lee v. Weisman*, 1992

JUSTICE DAVIS SOUTER
We are three centuries away from the St. Bartholomew's Day massacre and the treatment of heretics in early Massachusetts, but the divisiveness of religion in current public life is inescapable. This is no time to deny the prudence of understanding the Establishment Clause to require the Government to stay neutral on religious belief, which is reserved for the conscience of the individual.—Majority Opinion, *McCreary County, Ky. v. ACLU of Kentucky* ("the Ten Commandments ruling"), June 27, 2005

5.

Notable Americans' Fighting Words on Church v. State, and on Religion v. Spirituality

Given the current religious-revival climate, and the tendency to demonize critics of "theocracy politics," it's vital to understand that the United States has a long, honorable history of such critiques. Not only have the Founders, elected officials, and distinguished jurists strongly affirmed the separation of church and state.

Major, "mainstream" American figures of both genders and every ethnicity—in politics, literature, the arts, science, law, philosophy, social-justice movements (slavery abolition, women's suffrage, civil rights, etc.), even in the clergy itself—have gone on record about this issue. They have also been public about their varying rejections of organized, hierarchical, religious establishments in favor of other, freer forms of spirituality, and their preference for actions rather than rituals to address human suffering. Many suffered public denunciation, some endured prison sentences or banishment. The nineteenth-century women's movement (focused on abolition of slavery, women's suffrage, critiques of the Bible, and more) was rife with "free-thinking" women, who were not only attacked as "infidels" like free-thinking men, but additionally branded "harlots," "whores," and "Jezebels." (Annie L. Gaylor's superb anthology, *Women Without Superstition*, cited in the section titled After Words, is a rich trove of these women's words—some published for the first time.) The list that follows (in this case, alphabetical, for reader convenience) is only a sampler of quotes from some of these distinguished Americans. For space reasons and to enhance ease of reading, I have included sourcing only for difficult-to-find citations. Other sources are easily located—via the resources in After Words.

Paula Gunn Allen 1939– (Pueblo/Sioux poet, Native American activist)

For the American Indian, the ability of all creatures to share in the process of ongoing creation makes all things sacred.

Susan B. Anthony 1820–1906 (women's suffrage leader, reformer)

I was born a heretic. I distrust those people who know so well what God wants them to do, because I notice it always coincides with their own desires.

Gloria Anzaldua 1942–2004 (Tejana-Chicana, feminist-lesbian poet)

I am playing with myself,
I am playing with the world's soul,

I am the dialogue between myself and *el espiritu del mundo*.

I change myself,

I change the world.

Isaac Asimov 1920–1992 (writer, futurist)

I am an atheist, out and out. It took me a long time to say it.

James Baldwin 1924–1987 (writer)

If the concept of God has any validity or any use, it can only be to make us larger, freer, and more loving. If God cannot do this, then it is time we got rid of Him.

Black Elk 1863–1950 (Oglala Sioux elder)

Everything an Indian does is in a circle. . . . The wind, in its greatest power, whirls. Birds make their nest in circles, for theirs is the same religion as ours.

Pearl Buck 1892–1973 (writer)

I am so absorbed in the wonder of earth and the life upon it that I cannot think of heaven and the angels.

George Carlin 1937– (comedian)

I'm completely in favor of the separation of Church and State . . . these two institutions screw us up enough on their own, so both of them together is certain death.

Charlie Chaplin 1889–1977 (actor, filmmaker)

By simple common sense I don't believe in God, in none.

Sandra Cisneros 1954– (writer)

I tell people I am a "Buddhalupist." I have to invent it, take parts of the Catholic religion that work for me, like the Virgin of Guadalupe, and toss out parts that don't.

Mary Daly 1928– (philosopher)

Why indeed must "God" be a noun? Why not a verb—the most active and dynamic of all?

"God's plan" is often a front for men's plans and a cover for inadequacy, ignorance, and evil.

John C. Danforth 1936– (Episcopal minister, former U.S. senator from Missouri, former U.S. ambassador to the UN)

We Republicans have allowed [our] shared agenda to become secondary to the agenda of Christian conservatives . . . a party that has gone so far in adopting a sectarian agenda that it's become the political extension of a religious movement. When government becomes the means of carrying out a religious program, it raises obvious questions under the First Amendment. But even in the absence of constitutional issues, a political party should resist identification with a religious movement. . . . At best, religion can be a uniting influence; in practice, nothing is more divisive.

Clarence Darrow 1857–1938 (attorney)

I do not consider it an insult, but rather a compliment, to be called an agnostic. I do not pretend to know where many ignorant men are sure . . . that is all that agnosticism means.

Emily Dickinson 1830–1886 (poet)

Some keep the Sabbath going to Church—
I keep it staying at home—
With a bobolink for a Chorister—
And an orchard for a Dome.

Frederick Douglass 1818–1895 (abolitionist leader)

I find . . . that I have, in several instances, spoken in such a tone and manner, respecting religion, as may possibly lead those unacquainted with my religious views to suppose me an opponent of all religion. . . . What I have said respecting and against religion, I mean strictly to apply to the *slaveholding* religion of this land. . . . Dark and terrible as is this picture, I hold it to be strictly true of the overwhelming mass of professed Christians in America. . . . They would be shocked at the proposition of fellowshipping a *sheep-stealer*, and at the same time they hug to their communion a *man-stealer*, and brand me with being an Infidel, if I find fault with them for it.

Theodore Dreiser 1871–1945 (writer, reformer)

If I were personally to define religion, I would say that it is a bandage that man has invented to protect a soul made bloody by circumstances.

W. E. B. Du Bois 1868–1941 (African American liberation leader)

I increasingly regarded the church as an institution which defended such evils as slavery, color caste, exploitation of labor, and war.

Thomas Alva Edison 1847–1931 (inventor)

Nature made us—nature did it all—not the gods of the religions. (*New York Times*, October 2, 1910)

Albert Einstein 1879–1955 (physicist)

It was, of course, a lie what you read about my religious convictions, a lie which is being systematically repeated. I do not believe in a personal God and I have never denied this but have expressed it clearly. If something is in me which can be called religious then it is the unbounded admiration for the structure of the world so far as our science can reveal it. (Letter, March 1954, *Albert Einstein: The Human Side*, eds. Helen Dukas and Banesh Hoffman, Princeton University Press)

Ralph Waldo Emerson 1803–1882 (ordained Unitarian minister, philosopher, writer)

God builds his temple in the heart, on the ruins of churches and religions.

Samuel James Ervin Jr. 1896–1985 (U.S. senator and judge)

Political freedom cannot exist in any land where religion controls the state, and religious freedom cannot exist in any land where the state controls religion.

Geraldine Ferraro 1935– (U.S. congresswoman, vice presidential nominee)

Personal religious convictions have no place in political campaigns or in dictating public policy.

Margaret Fuller 1810–1850 (writer, critic, Transcendentalist philosopher)

Let men who can with sincerity live in [the church]. I would not—for I believe far more widely than any body of men I know. . . . The blue sky seen above from the opposite roof preaches better than any brother.

Matilda Joslyn Gage 1826–1898 (suffragist, author of *Woman, Church, and State*)

Of late, a rapidly increasing tendency has been shown

towards the destruction of our civil liberties. . . . The government is undergoing changes which are signs of danger. They [the people] forget that liberty must ever be guarded. They forget the hereditary enslavement, the bondage of the human will to the church. . . . These are dangerous signs of the times as to the effort of the church to obtain increased power over the laity. It is also an attack of the church upon the state. (Speech at the Women's National Liberal Convention, 1890)

William Lloyd Garrison 1805–1879 (abolitionist, reformer, newspaper editor)

If the State cannot survive the . . . agitation, then let the State perish. If the Church must be cast down by the strugglings of Humanity to be free, then let the American Union be consumed by a living thunderbolt, and no tear shed over its ashes.

Charlotte Perkins Gilman 1860–1935 (author, *Woman and Economics* and *His Religion and Hers*)

[Let us inquire] what glory there was in an omnipotent being torturing forever a puny little creature who could in no way defend himself? Would it be to the glory of a man to fry ants?

Emma Goldman 1869–1940 (radical reformer)

I do not believe in God, because I believe in Man [*sic*].

Barry Goldwater 1909–1998 (conservative Republican senator from Arizona; presidential nominee)

The religious factions that are growing throughout our land are . . . trying to force government leaders into following their position 100 percent. If you disagree with these religious groups . . . they threaten you with a loss of money or votes or both. I'm frankly sick and tired of the political preachers across this country telling me as a citizen that if I want to be a moral person, I must believe in A, B, C, and D. Just who do they think they are? . . . I am even more angry as a legislator who must endure the threats of every religious group who thinks it has some God-granted right to control my vote on every roll call in the Senate. *I am warning them today: I will fight them every step of the way if they try to dictate their moral convictions to all Americans in the name of conservatism.* Religious factions will go on imposing their will on others unless decent people connected to them recognize that religion has no place in public policy.

Ernest Hemingway 1899–1961 (writer)

All thinking men are atheists.

Katharine Hepburn 1907–2003 (actor)

I'm an atheist, and that's it. I believe there's nothing we can know except that we should be kind to each other and do what we can for other people.

Robert Ingersoll 1833–1899 (lawyer, orator)

An infinite God ought to be able to protect Himself, without going in partnership with State Legislatures.

There are in nature neither rewards nor punishments, there are consequences.

William James 1842–1910 (psychologist, philosopher)

Religion is a monumental chapter in the history of human egotism.

Helen Keller 1880–1968 (writer, human-rights leader)

The heresy of one age becomes the orthodoxy of the next.

Dr. Martin Luther King Jr. 1929–1968 (Baptist minister, civil-rights leader, reformer)

The orthodox attempt to explain the divinity of Jesus in terms of an inherent metaphysical substance within him seems to me quite inadequate. . . . actually harmful and detrimental. To invest this Christ with such supernatural qualities makes the rejoinder: "Oh, well, he had a better chance for that kind of life than we can possible have." In other words, one could easily use this as a means to hide behind his failures. So that the orthodox view of the divinity of Christ is in my mind quite readily denied. ("The Humanity and Divinity of Jesus," 1950)

Maxine Hong Kingston 1940– (writer)

I learned to make my mind large, as the universe is large, so that there is room for paradoxes.

Reverend John Leland (eighteenth-century Baptist evangelist who supported Jefferson and Madison in securing the Virginia Act of Religious Freedom)

Let every man speak freely without fear, maintain the principles that he believes, worship according to his own faith, either one God, three Gods, no God, or twenty Gods; and let government protect him in doing so.

Butterfly McQueen 1911–1995 (actor)

As my ancestors are free from slavery, I am free from the slavery of religion.

If we had put the energy on earth and on people that

we put on mythology and on Jesus Christ, we wouldn't
have any hunger or homelessness.
Margaret Mead 1908–1978 (anthropologist)

We will be a better country when each religious group
can trust its members to obey the dictates of their own
religious faith without assistance from the legal structure
of their country.
Herman Melville 1819–1891 (writer)

Are there no Moravians in the Moon, that not a mis-
sionary has yet visited this poor pagan planet of ours, to
civilize civilization and christianize Christianity?
Senator Barbara Mikulski 1936– (Democrat, Maryland, speaking against the Federal Marriage Amendment, 2004)

No law, not a federal law, not a state law can force . . .
any religious institution to marry a same-sex couple.
That will be up to their religious determination. Why?
Because again, under separation of church and state, we
cannot dictate what a church does. Because of this Constitutional commitment, there can be no federal law, for
example, under equal opportunity, that could force the
Catholic Church to ordain women.
Toni Morrison 1931– (writer, Nobel Prize awardee)

As assaults on and demands for school prayer, religious symbols on school property, control of course cur-
ricula become legal cases . . . invoking the separation of
state and church, that legal journey both skirts and displays another question. . . . Which values, in act or
symbol, should a public institution of learning reject,

endorse, or tolerate? . . . Why should schools close on religious holidays? Why should they be called *holi* as in holy days? Why permit houses of worship to participate in school and academic functions? I am merely suggesting how porous the "separation" of church and state is. . . . These are the Great Debates of the twenty-first century . . . whether our, or any, notion of secular morality is "universal." Whether whole bodies of knowledge are secret agendas of oppression.

Lucretia Mott 1793-1880 (Quaker heretic, abolitionist, women's' suffrage leader)

I resolved to claim for my sex all that an impartial creator had bestowed, which, by custom and a perverted application of the scriptures, had been wrested from woman.

Bill Moyers 1934 (ordained minister, journalist, social commentator)

The Religious Right drowned everyone else out. And they hijacked Jesus.

Louis Nizer 1902–1994 (attorney)

Believing in gods always causes confusion.

Senator Barack Obama 1961– (Democrat, Illinois)

The difficult thing about any religion, including Christianity, is that at some level there is a call to evangelize and proselytize.

I'm a big believer in the separation of church and state. I am a big believer in our constitutional structure.

Elaine Pagels 1943– (religion scholar)

There's practically no religion I know of that sees other people in a way that affirms the other's choice.

Edgar Allan Poe 1809–1849 (writer)

All religion . . . is simply evolved out of chicanery, fear, greed, imagination, and poetry.

Gene Roddenberry 1921–1991 (television writer/ producer: *Star Trek*)

Religions vary in their degree of idiocy, but I reject them all. For most people, religion is nothing more than a substitute for a malfunctioning brain.

Eleanor Roosevelt 1884–1962 (human-rights leader, journalist, First Lady)

I do not want church groups controlling the schools of our country. They must remain free. (*My Day* column, July 8, 1949)

The separation of church and state is extremely important to any of us who holds to the original traditions of our nation. (New York *World-Telegram*, June 23, 1949)

Ernestine Rose 1810–1892 (immigrant from a Polish Jewish ghetto, first U.S. lobbyist for women's rights, self-proclaimed atheist)

All children are atheists, and were religion not inculcated into their minds they would remain so.

Carl Sagan 1934–1996 (astronomer)

For all our conceits about being the center of the universe, we live in a routine planet of a humdrum star stuck away in an obscure corner . . . on an unexceptional galaxy which is one of about 100 billion galaxies. . . . That is the fundamental fact of the universe we inhabit, and it is very good for us to understand that.

Margaret Sanger 1879–1966 (reproductive-rights pioneer)

No Gods No Masters (motto of her newspaper, *The Woman Rebel*, 1914)

George Santayana 1863–1952 (philosopher)

My atheism, like that of Spinoza, is true piety towards the universe and denies only gods fashioned by men in their own image to be servants of their human interests.

Representative Christopher Shays 1945– (Republican, Connecticut)

This Republican Party of Lincoln has become a party of theocracy. There are going to be repercussions.

Upton Sinclair 1878–1968 (writer, reformer)

The first thing brought forth by the study of any religion, ancient or modern, is that it is based upon Fear. . . . Man is an evasive beast, given to cultivating strange notions about himself. He is humiliated by his simian ancestry. (*The Profits of Religion*, 1918)

Elizabeth Cady Stanton 1815–1902

[*Note:* Stanton, the great radical writer and visionary of the nineteenth-century women's movement (and author of the text of the Nineteenth Amendment to the Constitution), wrote extensively about religion's effect on women's status. The samples below are from her audacious book *The Woman's Bible* (1895, 1898), her "The Degraded Status of Women in the Bible" (1896), various diary entries (1882, 1895), her *Letters*, and her autobiography, *Eighty Years and More* (1898).]

The Bible and the church have been the greatest stumbling blocks in the way of women's emancipation. . . . [teaching] that woman brought sin and death into the world. . . . Marriage for her was to be a condition of bondage, maternity a period of suffering and anguish, and in silence and subjection, she was to play the role of a dependent on man's bounty for all her material wants.

Jehovah has never taken a very active part in the suffrage movement.

For fifty years the women of this nation have tried to dam up this deadly stream that poisons all their lives, but thus far they have lacked the insight or courage to follow it back to its source and there strike the blow at the fountain of all tyranny: religious superstition, priestly power, and the canon law.

I have been in many of the ancient cathedrals—grand, wonderful, mysterious. But I always leave them with a feeling of indignation because of the generations of human beings who struggled in poverty to build these altars to the unknown god.

I asked them why . . . one read in the synagogue service every week the "I thank thee, o lord, that I was not born a woman." "It is not meant in an unfriendly spirit intended to degrade or humiliate women" [was their response]. . . . Suppose the service read "I thank thee o lord that I was not born a jackass." Could that be twisted in any way into a compliment to the jackass?

The greatest obstacle we [suffragists] had to overcome was the Bible. It was hurled at us on every side.

Amy Tan 1952– (writer, Asian American activist)

In losing my Christian faith what I really lost was the

idea of a set of beliefs handed to me, and what I look for now is spiritual beliefs.

Sojourner Truth (nineteenth-century abolitionist and suffragist leader)

Religion without humanity is poor human stuff.

That little man in black says woman can't have as much rights as man because Christ wasn't a woman. Where did your Christ come from? . . . From God and a woman. Man has nothing to do with him.

Mark Twain (Samuel Clemens) 1835–1910 (writer)

[*Note:* Twain's writings on religion are so numerous that these samples are tips of a field of icebergs. See his *Reflections on Religion*, *Letters from the Earth*, and the great, scathing *The War Prayer*—about which he noted "I have told the whole truth in that, and only dead men can tell the truth in this world. It can be published after I am dead," which it was, in 1923.]

Faith is believing what you know ain't so.

It ain't the parts of the Bible that I can't understand that bother me, it is the parts that I do understand.

Life itself is only a vision and a dream, for nothing exists but space and you. If there was an all-powerful God, he would have made all good and no bad.

Our Bible reveals to us the character of our god with minute and remorseless exactness. . . . It is perhaps the most damnatory biography that exists in print anywhere. It makes Nero an angel of light and leading by contrast.

If there is a God, he is a malign thug.

O Lord our God, help us tear their soldiers to bloody shreds with our shells.

Jane Wagner 1935– (writer)

Why is it when we talk to God, we're said to be praying—but when God talks to us, we're schizophrenic? . . . One thing I have no worry about is whether God exists. But it has occurred to me that God has Alzheimer's and has forgotten we exist. *(The Search for Intelligent Life in the Universe,* performed by **Lily Tomlin**, 1986)

Alice Walker 1944– (writer)

Any God I ever felt in church I brought in with me.

Jessamyn West 1903–1984 (writer)

Friends [Quakers] refused to take legal oaths, since by doing so they acquiesced in the assumption that, unless under oath, one was not obliged to tell the truth.

Roger Williams 1603–1684 (Church of England minister)

[*Note:* Roger Williams was tried, convicted, and banished by Puritan elders from the Massachusetts Bay Colony; in 1631 he founded Rhode Island on principles of religious tolerance and church-state separation, thereby influencing Jefferson.]

No person should be restrained from, nor constrained to, any worship or ministry, except in accordance with the dictates of his own conscience.

God requireth not an uniformity of Religion to be inacted and inforced in any civill state.

Sarah Winnemuca (eighteenth-century Paiute Native American rights activist)

(To an Indian agent): Hell is full of just such Christians as you are.

Frances Wright 1795–1852 (abolitionist, suffragist, lecturer)

Time is it to arrest our speculations respecting unseen worlds and inconceivable mysteries, and to address our inquiries to the improvement of the human condition . . . those beautiful principles of liberty and equality enshrined in the political institutions and, first and in chief, in the national declaration of independence.

I am neither Jew nor Gentile, Mahomedan nor Theist; I am but a member of the human family.

Frank Lloyd Wright 1869–1959 (architect)

I believe in God, only I spell it Nature.

6.

Abortion:
The Fighting Word?

At first glance, this chapter may not seem to be as directly related as the others are to the issue of church-state separation. But it cannot be excluded, since a woman's right to choose is and has been for decades *the* flashpoint issue for discussions of religious incursions into government.

The religious right's position on abortion has been consistently antagonistic, and their well-financed crusade—state-by-state as well as federal—has been carefully planned and enacted over three decades. Their tactics have ranged from sophisticated lobbying and public relations campaigns to flat-out terrorism: bombing clinics and murdering medical staff. They have skillfully used this issue as a fund-raising tool; as a political wedge to field, fund, and elect candidates; and as a hammer to chip steadily away at *Roe v. Wade*—via pressure for executive

presidential orders, (contested) legislation outlawing
emergency abortion, demands for parental notification,
and so forth. Their attacks on Supreme Court decisions
plus their efficient political organizing have managed, as I
write this, to put two more extreme conservatives on the
Court, men who flatly refused during Senate confirmation
hearings to state any respect for the legal precedent of *Roe*.
Their rhetorical and active attempts to intimidate through
violence have been so frighteningly successful that they
almost don't need to bother with overturning *Roe* formally:
today, in 2006, fewer U.S. medical schools require profi-
ciency in pregnancy termination—and *86 percent of all U.S.
counties have no abortion provider whatsoever.*

The Protestant religious right's position is based primarily on that of the Roman Catholic Church, since the
Bible does *not* forbid the procedure. Furthermore, while
there are a few subtle differences among the opposition
—one or two groups, for instance, permit (some) contra-
ceptive use—but a growing number would silence even
information about contraception, much less make it available. All of them claim that their religious convictions
alone "serve the state's interest."

So it is relevant indeed to address this subject and to
replace the untruths, half-truths, and outright lies with
some simple facts.

For example:

   1. *There is no mention of abortion as a crime or as a
      woman's right in the United States Constitution.*
      This is because:

a) There is no mention of *women* in the Constitution.

b) Abortion was both legal and practiced at the time.

2. *There is no mention of abortion in the Bible.*

There are as many as six hundred Mosaic laws, but not one comments on abortion. Jewish law traditionally considers that life begins at birth. Exodus 21:22–25 refers to miscarriage due to a woman being hurt accidentally as men fight— adding that the culprit should be fined, but if the *woman* (*not* the fetus) dies, he should be killed. In general, the Bible is not particularly child-friendly, murdering the firstborn of every Egyptian household (Exodus 12:29), ordering that infants of adversaries should be "dashed to pieces" (Hosea 13:16), "ripped up" (II Kings, 8:12), "slain" (I Samuel 15:3), and "eaten" (Deuteronomy 28:53), and so forth. Psalm 137:9 proclaims, "Happy shall he be, that taketh and dasheth thy little ones against the stones."

3. The history of the Roman Catholic Church's position—from which current U.S. antichoice extremist Christian positions derive—is not what you think. Today's Vatican finds even the words "reproductive health" unacceptable in official United Nations documents—in case anyone might construe them to include the already deleted word "abortion"—and it lobbies effectively

(in coalition with Islamists and Protestant funda-
mentalists) to purge all UN documents of such
language.

*But the Catholic Church's opposition to abortion was not
always so absolute.*

It was only in 1869 that abortion at any stage was
made subject to automatic excommunication. This had
to do with the church's position on *sexuality*, not respect
for fetal life. The church pretends that its position on
abortion has been based on a "right to life" and has
remained unchanged for two thousand years. In fact, it
has varied continually over the course of history, with no
unanimous opinion on the subject at any one time.

In 400 C.E., Augustine expressed the then-mainstream
view that early abortion required penance only for the
sexual aspect of the sin, *not* as homicide; eight hundred
years later, Thomas Aquinas substantially agreed.

Between 1198 and 1216, Pope Innocent III ruled
abortion as "not irregular" if the fetus was not "vivified"
or "animated"; animation was considered eighty days
for a female and forty days for a male—though it was
not explained how anyone could tell the difference in
the womb.

Pope Sixtus V forbade all abortions in 1588, but in
1591 Pope Gregory XIV rescinded that order, reestab-
lishing permission to abort up to forty days for both a
male or female fetus.

(Saint) Antoninus, Archbishop of Florence, a
fifteenth-century Dominican who wrote a major treatise

on abortion, taught that *early abortion to save a woman's life was moral.*

Thomas Sanchez, a seventeenth-century Jesuit, noted that all his Catholic theologian contemporaries *justified* abortion to save the life of the woman.

It was only in 1869 that Pius IX ruled all abortion murder and defined it as an excommunicable sin. Some scholars argue that this edict was issued under pressure from Napoleon III, who was concerned that the birthrate had been dropping and that France might face a serious depletion of soldiers for its wars and colonizations. Furthermore, and also contrary to popular belief, *the prohibition of abortion is not governed by claims of papal infallibility,* which leaves more far room for discussion than is usually assumed.

If this issue isn't governed by infallibility, and if the church position itself has been flexible, and if there is no mention of forbidding abortion in the Bible or the Constitution, then just how and why *is* this issue so explosive in discussing the separation of church and state?

7.

In *Other* Words: The Opposition

Abandon complacency, all ye who enter here.

Why include a section on extreme religious right quotes when such statements surround us every day? Well, if you thought you'd grasped the situation in the United States of America in the late twentieth and early twenty-first centuries, read on.

We are a nation of short memories. We like to think we've moved beyond the judge who, in 1959, declared that "Almighty God did not intend for the races to mix," in his justification of Virginia's ban on interracial marriage—yet it wasn't until *Loving v. Virginia* worked its way up to the Supreme Court, in 1967, that this law was overthrown. Meanwhile, back in the schoolrooms, stunning, deliberate miseducation continues, and not just in publicized issues, like "creationist" or "intelligent design" campaigns to overthrow scientific fact: *Elements of Literature for*

Christian Schools (Robert Horton, Donalynn Hess, and Steven Skeggs; Bob Jones University, 2001) denounces Mark Twain (as a defiant rebel) and Emily Dickinson (for viewing salvation as a gamble, not a certainty). This is one of many such textbooks—on history, economics, even physics (warning that "secular physics" will weaken a student's faith).

A few of the following samples may be familiar for being *so* outrageous that they merited media coverage. What is even more alarming are those that garnered little or no press attention For instance, many people (including some evangelicals) might dismiss Pat Robertson—with his calls for assassination of foreign leaders and for using nuclear bombs against non-Christian nations—as being so extreme or even mentally unbalanced that he has become an irrelevant joke. But it's no joke that his *The 700 Club* program reaches an average of one million households a day. Similarly, Americans laughed when Jerry Falwell denounced the cartoon characters "Teletubbies" as carrying "pro-gay" messages, and cited "the Biblical condemnation of feminism [which] has to do with its radical philosophy and goals." But as early as 1986, Falwell's so-called "Moral Majority" already had six million people on its mailing list, and it's been growing. No laughing matter.

So, to remind us all, here—chronologically and historically—is what our adversaries say, *in their own words*. We should, of course, start with the Bible itself, since political religionists cite it as the "fundamentals" on which they intend to model the laws of and life in the United States. A few examples must suffice:

Genesis 3:14: Snakes have no legs because Eve snacked on fruit.

Genesis 24:3; Numbers 25:1-9; Ezra 9:12; Nehemiah 10:30: Marriages of believers and nonbelievers are forbidden.

Genesis 29:17–28; II Samuel 3:2–5: Marriage is a union between one man and one—or more—women.

Genesis 38:6–10; Deuteronomy 25:5–10: When a married man dies childless, his widow must marry his brother. If the brother refuses, he must pay a fine of one shoe and be otherwise punished in a manner to be determined by law.

Exodus 21:7: When a man sells his daughter as a slave, she shall not go out free, though male slaves may; *and* 35:2: Any person who works on the Sabbath shall be put to death.

Leviticus 11: [Pork] flesh you shall not eat, and their dead bodies not touch [no gloves, mitts, or footballs]; *and* 12:2–6: After bearing a son, a woman must be ostracized as unclean for seven days; after bearing a daughter, for two weeks; *and* 18:22: Proscription against (male) homosexuality as "abomination": *and* 21:16–23: Proscriptions against disabled persons. Also, 21–23: Insects have four legs.

Deuteronomy 7:3: Proscriptions against interracial marriages *and* 22:22–29: Stoning for both a rapist and his victim—or a woman must marry her rapist; *and* 22:13–21: A marriage is valid only if the wife is a virgin; if she isn't, she must be executed by stoning, *and* Deuteronomy 22:19: There can be no divorce, *and* Mark 10:9 *and* I Corinthians 7:10–11: Still no divorce.

Ezekiel 7:2; Revelation 7:1: The earth is shaped like a rectangle.

Judges 11:30–39: It is permissible to slaughter and sacrifice a daughter as a burnt offering to the Lord (but a son must be saved—Genesis 22: Abraham and Isaac).

II Samuel 5:13; I Kings 11:3; II Chronicles 11:21: Marriage shall not impede a man's right to take concubines in addition to his wives.

Matthew 19:12: It is good to castrate yourself.

I Corinthians 7:1–40: Refrain from sex whenever possible, but (unless you are a bishop) multiple wives are fine (I Timothy 3:2, 12).

Luke 8:27: Devils cause mental illness.

And so forth and so on. . . .
Now, for a few words from real people.

CHRISTOPHER COLUMBUS

And I say that Your Highnesses ought not to consent that any foreigner does business or sets foot here [in the New World], except Christian Catholics, since this was the end and the beginning of the enterprise, that it should be for the enhancement and glory of the Christian religion, nor should anyone who is not a good Christian come to these parts. (*Journal of the First Voyage*, November 1492)

COTTON MATHER

I write the wonders of the Christian religion, flying from the depravations of Europe to the American strand: and assisted by the Holy Author of that religion, I . . . report the wonderful displays of His infinite power . . . wherewith his Divine Providence hath irradiated a savage Indian wilderness. (Introduction to *Magnalia Christi Americana*, 1702)

PATRICK HENRY

I hear it is said by the Deists that I am one of the number; and indeed, that some good people think I am no Christian. This thought gives me much more pain than the appellation of Tory; because I think religion of infinitely higher importance than politics. (Letter, August 20, 1796)

REVEREND BIRD WILSON
(EPISCOPAL MINISTER)

The founders of our nation were [disappointingly] nearly all Infidels, and that of the presidents thus far elected not a one has professed a belief in Christianity . . . among all our presidents from Washington downward, not one was a professor of religion—at least not of more than Unitarianism. (Interview, *The New York Times*, November 1831)

TEXAS GOVERNOR
MIRIAM "MA" FERGUSON

If English was good enough for Jesus Christ, it's good enough for Texas. (Announcement while brandishing a Bible, after outlawing the teaching of foreign languages in Texas, in the 1920s)

But enough of the past. Here is *recent* history—as it was carefully planned and constructed—into the present.

PAUL WEYRICH (FOUNDER, THE HERITAGE FOUNDATION)

We are talking about Christianizing America. We are talking about the Gospel in a political context. (Speech, Free Congress Foundation, August 1980)

JAMES G. WATT (FORMER U.S. SECRETARY OF THE INTERIOR)

My responsibility is to follow the Scriptures which call upon us to occupy the land until Jesus returns. (Quoted in *The Washington Post*, May 24, 1981)

GARY NORTH
(CHRISTIAN POLITICAL THEORIST)

We must use the doctrine of religious liberty to gain independence for Christian schools until we train up a generation of people who know that there is no religious neutrality, no neutral law, no neutral education, and no neutral civil government. Then they will get busy constructing a Bible-based social, political, and religious order. ("The Intellectual Schizophrenia of the New Christian Right" in *Christianity and Civilization: The Failure of the American Baptist Culture*, no. 1 [spring, 1982])

GARY POTTER (PRESIDENT, CATHOLICS
FOR CHRISTIAN POLITICAL ACTION)

After the Christian majority takes control, pluralism will be seen as immoral and evil and the state will not permit anybody the right to practice evil. (Cited in *Holy Terror: The Fundamentalist War on America's Freedoms in Religion, Politics, and Our Private Lives*, Flo Conway and Jim Siegelman, eds., New York, Dell, 1984)

REVEREND PAT ROBERTSON

The Constitution of the United States, for instance, is a marvelous document for self-government by the Christian people. But the minute you turn the document into the hands of non-Christian people and atheistic people they can use it to destroy the very foundation of our society. (*The 700 Club* TV program, December 30, 1981)

The termites are in charge now, and that is not the

way it ought to be, and the time has arrived for a godly fumigation. (*New York Magazine*, August 18, 1986)

I don't think the Congress of the United States is subservient to the courts. . . . They can ignore a Supreme Court ruling if they so choose. (Statement to *The Washington Post* editorial board, June 27, 1986)

You're supposed to be nice to the Episcopalians and the Presbyterians and the Methodists and this, that, and the other thing. Nonsense. I don't have to be nice to the spirits of the Antichrist. (*The 700 Club*, January 14, 1991)

By the end of this decade, if we work and give and organize and train, the Christian Coalition will be the most powerful political organization in America. (Fundraising letter, July 4, 1991)

Expect confrontations that will be not only unpleasant but at times physically bloody. . . . Institutions will be plunged into wrenching change. . . . When it is over, I am convinced God's people will emerge victorious. (Pat Robertson's *Perspective Octavo*, 1992)

The feminist agenda is not about equal rights for women. It is about a socialist, anti-family political movement that encourages women to leave their husbands, kill their children, practice witchcraft, destroy capitalism, and become lesbians. (*The Washington Post*, August 23, 1993)

We can change education in America if you put Christian principles and Christian pedagogy in. In three years, you would totally revolutionize education in America. (*The 700 Club*, September 27, 1993)

They have kept us in submission because they have talked about separation of church and state. There is no such thing in the Constitution. It's a lie of the left, and we're not going to take it anymore. (Speech, November 14, 1993)

BEVERLY LAHAYE (PRESIDENT, CONCERNED WOMEN FOR AMERICA)
Yes, religion and politics do mix. America is a nation based on Biblical principles. Politicians who do not use the bible to guide their public and private lives do not belong in office. (Quoted in *Ms.*, February 1987)

GEORGE HERBERT WALKER BUSH (FORTY-FIRST U.S. PRESIDENT)
No, I don't know that atheists should be considered as citizens, nor should they be considered as patriots. This is one nation under God. (Interview, *American Atheist*, August 27, 1987)

CHARLES W. "CHUCK" COLSON (CONVICTED 1973 OF OBSTRUCTING JUSTICE IN WATERGATE SCANDAL; BORN-AGAIN CHRISTIAN FOUNDER OF PRISON FELLOWSHIP ORGANIZATION)
Indeed, the time has come for Congress to call into question the very legitimacy of the Supreme Court's status as sole and final arbiter of what the Constitution means. ("Whose Constitution Is It Anyway?" June 26, 1997)

REVEREND JERRY FALWELL

The idea that religion and politics don't mix was invented by the Devil to keep Christians from running our own country. (Sermon, July 4, 1976)

In the next ten years, I trust that we will have more Christian day schools than there are public schools. I hope I will live to see the day when, as in the early days of our country, we won't have any public schools. The churches will have taken them over again and Christians will be running them. (*America Can Be Saved*, 1979)

If we are going to save America and evangelize the world, we cannot accommodate secular philosophies. ("Moral Majority Report," September, 1984)

I really believe that the pagans, and the abortionists, and the feminists, and the gays and lesbians who are actively trying to make that an alternative lifestyle. . . . I point the finger in their face and say "you helped this [9/11 attack] happen. (*The 700 Club*, September 13, 2001)

GARY BAUER
(PRESIDENT OF AMERICAN VALUES,
FORMER PRESIDENTIAL CANDIDATE)

I feel uncomfortable that good Christians all over America, and indeed the world, are using a document [the King James Bible] commissioned by a homosexual [King James I of England, in 1611]. Anything that has been commissioned by a homosexual has obviously been tainted in some way. . . . Christians should cease using the translation and instead use a recent version, such as

"The Good News Bible." (Press conference of Family Research Council, Christian Coalition, and Americans for Truth about Homosexuality, 1999)

RANDALL TERRY (HEAD OF "OPERATION RESCUE," MILITANT ANTI-CHOICE GROUP)

[Supreme Court Justices] Blackmun and Stevens are enemies of Christ. (*Christianity Today*, September 10, 1990)

I want you to let a wave of hatred wash over you. Yes, hate is good. . . . Our goal is a Christian nation. We have a biblical duty, we are called on by God to conquer this country. We don't want equal time. We don't want pluralism. (Quoted in *News Sentinel*, Ft. Wayne, Indiana, August 16, 1993)

PATRICK BUCHANAN (FORMER PRESIDENTIAL CANDIDATE, CONSERVATIVE PUNDIT)

Gay rights activists seek to substitute, for laws rooted in Judeo-Christian morality, laws rooted in the secular humanist belief that all consensual sexual acts are morally equal. (Quoted in The *Wall Street Journal*, January 21, 1993)

We're going to bring back God and the Bible and drive the gods of secular humanism right out of the public schools of America. (Speech, Des Moines, Iowa, February 11, 1996)

CAL THOMAS

We are approaching a time when Christians, especially, may have to declare the social contract between

Enlightenment rationalists and Biblical believers—which formed the basis of the Constitution written at our nation's founding—null and void. (*The Washington Times*, October 23, 1996)

SAM SILLIGATO

[When] the mythical wall of separation is removed, thousands will be able to learn of America's true Christian heritage and the principles and morals that this heritage has bestowed. (Salvation Army publication *The War Cry*, 1998)

JANET PARSHALL

A religion that doesn't discriminate wouldn't exist, because it wouldn't stand for anything. (Family Research Council's "Washington Watch Radio Commentary," September 1, 2000)

GEORGE W. BUSH (FORTY-THIRD U.S. PRESIDENT)

Therefore, I, George W. Bush, Governor of Texas, do hereby proclaim June 10, 2000, "Jesus Day" in Texas and urge the appropriate recognition whereof. In official recognition whereof, I hereby affix my signature this 17th day of April, 2000.

God wants me to run for President. I know it won't be easy on me or my family, but God wants me to do it. (Campaign statement, 2000, to Texas evangelist James Robinson)

I fully understand that the job of the president is and must always be protecting the great right of people to worship or not worship as they see fit. That's what distinguishes us from the Taliban. On the other hand, I don't see how you can be president, without a relationship with the Lord. . . . What we are going to do in the second term is make sure that grant money is available for faith communities to bid on. . . . *But the key thing is, is that we do have the capacity to allow faith programs to access enormous sums of social service money.* (Press conference, 2005)

THE PRESIDENTIAL PRAYER TEAM

Pray for the President as he seeks wisdom on how to legally codify the definition of marriage. Pray that it will be according to Biblical principles. With many forces insisting on variant definitions of marriage, pray that God's Word and His standards will be honored by our government. (www.presidentialprayerteam.org)

TEXAS REPUBLICAN PARTY PLATFORM, 2002

Our Party pledges to do everything within its power to dispel the myth of separation of church and state.

TOM DELAY (INDICTED; FORMER HOUSE MAJORITY LEADER, FORMER CON-GRESSMAN, REPUBLICAN—TEXAS)

[The Faith-Based Initiative is a way of] standing up and rebuking this notion of separation of church and state that has been imposed upon us over the last 40 or 50 years. (Speech at a luncheon for congressional staff in July 2001)

We set up the courts. We can unset the courts. (Comments on court ruling, 2005)

JEB BUSH (GOVERNOR OF FLORIDA)

I can't think of a better place to reflect on the awesome love of our Lord Jesus than to be here at Lawtey Correctional. (Speech dedicating the nation's first religion-based prison, in Florida; quoted in *The New York Times*, December 25, 2003)

JAMES DOBSON (FOUNDER, FOCUS ON THE FAMILY)

[Homosexuality] will destroy marriage. It will destroy the Earth. (Oklahoma political rally, October 22, 2004)

COMPETITORS' CREED, FROM THE FELLOWSHIP OF CHRISTIAN ATHLETES

I am a Christian first and last

I am created in the likeness of God Almighty to bring Him Glory

I am a member of Team Jesus Christ

I wear the colors of the cross

WILLIAM REHNQUIST (LATE CHIEF JUSTICE OF THE U.S. SUPREME COURT)

The "wall of separation between church and state" is a metaphor based on bad history, a metaphor which has proved useless as a guide to judging. It should be frankly and explicitly abandoned. (Dissent, *Wallace v. Jaffree*, 1985)

ANTONIN SCALIA
(U.S. SUPREME COURT JUSTICE)

[W]e have held that intentional governmental advancement of religion is sometimes required by the Free Exercise Clause. (Dissent, *Edwards v. Aguillard*, 1987)

The censorship of creation science . . . deprives students of knowledge of one of the two scientific explanations for the origin of life and leads them to believe that evolution is proven fact; thus, their education suffers and they are wrongly taught that science has proved their religious beliefs false. (Dissent, *Edwards v. Aguillard*, 1987)

The Constitution that I interpret is not living but dead. . . . [The principle of separation of church and state] is not imbedded in the Constitution. (Speech at Religious Freedom Day, January 12, 2003)

[It is a] demonstrably false principle that the government cannot favor religion over irreligion. . . . With respect to public acknowledgment of religious belief, it is entirely clear from our Nation's historical practices that the Establishment Clause permits this disregard of polytheists and believers in unconcerned deities, just as it permits the disregard of devout atheists. (Dissenting opinion, *McCreary County, Ky. v. ACLU of Kentucky* ("the Ten Commandments ruling," 2005)

CLARENCE THOMAS
(U.S. SUPREME COURT JUSTICE)

We can see no logical difference in kind between the invocation of Christianity by the Club and the invocation of teamwork, loyalty, or patriotism by other associations to provide a foundation for their lessons. (*Good News Club v. Milford Central Schools*, 2001)

STATE REPRESENTATIVE DON DAVIS
(REPUBLICAN—NORTH CAROLINA)

Two things made this country great: White men & Christianity. The degree these two have diminished is in direct proportion to the corruption and fall of the nation. Every problem . . . can be directly traced back to our departure from God's Law and the disenfranchisement of White men. (E-mailed to all members of the North Carolina House and Senate, reported by *The Fayetteville Observer*, August 22, 2001)

JOHN ASHCROFT (FORMER SENATOR,
REPUBLICAN—MISSOURI; FORMER U.S.
ATTORNEY GENERAL)

Because we have understood that our source is eternal, America has been different. We have no king but Jesus. (Address at Bob Jones University, May 8, 1999)

The voice of evil disguised as freedom whispers. (Address, National Religious Broadcasters Convention, Nashville, Tennessee, February 19, 2002)

ROY MOORE (FORMER ALABAMA SUPREME COURT CHIEF JUSTICE)

That phrase (separation of church and state) has so warped our society it's unbelievable. (Speech, Christian Coalition "Road to Victory" Convention, 2002)

REPRESENTATIVE JO ANN DAVIS (REPUBLICAN—VIRGINIA)

[Elected officials] must do what the scriptures say. God told me I would be in Congress, but gave me two words: "No compromise." (Speech, CC Convention, 2002)

REPRESENTATIVE ROBERT ADERHOLT (REPUBLICAN—ALABAMA)

We would make the argument, the Supreme Court does not always have the final authority over the interpretation of the Constitution. (Speech launching the "Ten Commandments Defense Act"—H. R. 3895, March 7, 2002)

LIEUTENANT GENERAL WILLIAM G. BOYKIN (FORMER UNDERSECRETARY OF DEFENSE)

The enemy will only be defeated if we come against them in the name of Jesus. . . . we're a Christian nation, because our foundation and our roots are Judeo-Christian and the enemy is a guy named Satan. . . . my God was bigger than his! (Speech, January 2003, Daytona, Florida)

Why is this man [George W. Bush] in the White House?

The majority of Americans did not vote for him. I tell you this morning that he's in the White House because God put him there for a time such as this. (Speech, June 2003)

WILLIAM DONAHUE (PRESIDENT OF THE CATHOLIC LEAGUE)

Mel Gibson represents the mainstream of America. (MSNBC's "Scarborough Country," December 8, 2004)

BILL O'REILLY (RADIO AND TV COMMENTATOR)

[I pick on] the ACLU because they're the most dangerous organization in the United States of America. They're, like, second next to Al Qaeda. (June 2, 2004 broadcast, "The Radio Factor")

RUSH LIMBAUGH (RADIO COMMENTATOR)

The International Red Cross is a joke. . . . *The New York Times* just hates this country. . . . Listen to what the *Times* reports as prisoner abuse at G'itmo. . . . "making uncooperative prisoners strip to their underwear, having them sit in a chair while shackled hand and foot to a bolt in the floor, and forcing them to endure strobe lights and loud rock and rap music played through two close loudspeakers while air-conditioning was turned up to maximum levels." Folks, that happens every night in New York City at any club you go into, except the underwear. (November 30, 2004, broadcast)

BISHOP HAROLD CALVIN RAY

The separation of church and state is a fiction. (February 2001 interview in *Charisma* magazine)

BISHOP MARVA MITCHELL

There's never been a separation of church and state. The only thing that's been separated is us from the money. (Statement after "Faith-Based Initiative" meeting with George W. Bush, 2005)

REVEREND BILL SHANKS (PASTOR, NEW COVENANT FELLOWSHIP OF NEW ORLEANS)

[Thanks to Hurricane Katrina] New Orleans now is abortion free. New Orleans now is Mardi Gras free. New Orleans now is free of Southern Decadence and the sodomites, the witchcraft workers, false religion, it's free of all of those things now. . . . Christians are God's authorized representatives on the face of the Earth. . . . (Sermon, 2005)

OHIO RESTORATION PROJECT (WWW.OHIORESTORATIONPROJECT.COM/ PLAN.PHP)

Organize and execute: 1) Pastor Policy Briefings in targeted cities: Cincinnati, Columbus, Cleveland, Canton/Akron, Dayton/Springfield, . . . identify and equip 2,000 Pastors to become Patriot Pastors. . . . OHIO

FOR JESUS Advertising—30-second radio spots fea-
turing Secretary of State Ken Blackwell on "The Stewardship of our Citizenship." . . . host 7 Pastor Policy Briefings
from March through September. . . . Marketing packets to
be distributed through these meetings . . . encourage ministers across the state to: preach and inform their congregations on issues relevant to the Christian Community . . .
build a network of addresses and e-mails that will equip
concerned Christians to become informed "Minutemen"
of our day. . . . build to a total of 300,000 on the mailing
list and 100,000 e-mail addresses. In a single day, we could
educate and mobilize hundreds of thousands who are able
to pray at a moment's notice. A Web site could be developed helping thousands of families to have access to information that equips these folks to make a stand. . . . Host
nonpartisan voter registration drives in churches. . . . 88
counties with more than 7,000 churches. If we could see
100,000 new registered voters involved in the process, this
would be a serious step towards the "Stewardship of our
Citizenship." . . . Voter Guides and inserts provided
from Christian Coalition, American Family Association, and Center For Moral Clarity. . . . Mobilize voter
participation . . . overall scope and sequence of these gath-
erings will be: Regional Policy Briefings (March through
September with 200–600 pastors at a time); Statewide
Patriot Pastors Gathering (late Oct.–early Nov. 2005 with
2,000+ pastors); Statewide OHIO FOR JESUS Rally
(Late Feb–Mid March, 2006); Regional Policy Briefings:

8 weeks prior [to elections]: Targeted Mailings, E-mail Announcements for their Regional Pastor's Policy Briefing. Then, 6 weeks prior: Pastor Russell will meet host church and key leaders to discuss program, speakers, details, and promotion for next Pastor's Policy Briefing. 6–4 weeks prior: Second mailing and e-mailing with more specifics. During this time registrations and follow up phone calls to be made. . . . We have invited 2,000+ Pastors and they will take Marketing Packets for the OHIO FOR JESUS Rally late February–early March. (This gives them enough time to go home and host Voter Registration days in March and April in time for the May primary.) In a 2–3 hour gathering: 25,000 people will leave Informed, Registered, Involved, Encouraging others to be involved. When the 2005–2006 cycle is completed, our goal will be to have accomplished: Christian Minutemen mailing list enlarged to 300,000 and 100,000 e-mails . . . 4 Million Voter Guides distributed fall 2005 for first the May Primaries in 2006, then for November 2006.

This disciplined count-down to election day in Ohio is happening in similar form in every other state. And it is happening right *now*. . . .

8.

After Words:
Resources for Action

GROUPS DEFENDING SEPARATION OF
CHURCH AND STATE (PARTIAL LIST)

American Humanist Association: www.americanhumanist.org

American Jewish Congress: www.ajc.org

American Muslim Perspective ("progressive Muslim organization"): www.amperspective.com

Americans United for Separation of Church and State:
www.au.org

Campaign to Defend the Constitution: www.DefCon
America.org

Catholics for Free Choice: www.catholicsforchoice.org

Clergy Leadership Network [or Clergy Laity Network]:
www.clnnlc.org ("a new interfaith movement of moderate and progressive clergy pursuing greater political
participation")

Constitutional Principle of Separation of Church and State:
    http://members.tripod.com/~candst/
Council on Secular Humanism: www.secularhumanism.org
Ethical Atheists: www.ethicalatheist.com
Feminist Majority Foundation: www.feminist.org
First Amendment Center: www.firstamendmentcenter.org
Freedom from Religion Foundation ("nontheists" and "free-
    thinkers" with a sense of humor: books, newsletter moni-
    toring the religious right, lawsuits, etc.): www.ffrf.org
Interfaith Alliance ("faith-based voice countering the radical
    right and promoting the positive role of religion."):
    www.interfaithalliance.org
Internet Infidels (Secular Web): www.infidels.org
Matilda Joslyn Gage Foundation: www.matildajoslyngage.org/
    religion.htm
National Council of Churches: www.ncccusa.org
National Organization for Women: www.now.org
People for the American Way:
    www.pfaw.org and savethecourt.org
Positive Atheism: www.positiveatheism.org
Religious Coalition for Reproductive Choice: info@rcrc.org
Revealer (daily review of religion and the press, published by
    NYU Department of Journalism and NYU Center for
    Religion and Media): www.therevealer.org
Secular Coalition for America: www.secular.org
Secular Student Alliance: www.secularstudents.org
Sister Fund: www.sisterfund.org
Sojourner Community: www.sojo.net ("progressive evangelical"
    group for "social justice")

Texas Freedom Network: www.tfn.org ("a mainstream voice to counter the religious right"); also, via same Web site: Texas Faith Network (coalition of progressive clergy)

Theocracy Watch (Project of the Center for Religion, Ethics, and Social Policy, Cornell University): www.theocracy-watch.org

United Church of Christ: www.ucc.org (supports women's ordination, same-sex marriage, civil rights; fields TV commercials confronting the Christian right)

[*Note:* Many national groups have state—sometimes even city—local chapters, and there are independent state-wide groups active as well. These can usually be located by Googling "separation church state groups _____" adding your state or city].

BOOKS AND ARTICLES

Allen, Ethan. *Reason the Only Oracle of Man.* New York: Scholars' Facsimiles and Reprints, 1940.

Brands, H. W. *Andrew Jackson: A Life and Times.* New York: Doubleday, 2005.

Chernow, Ron. *Alexander Hamilton.* New York: Penguin, 2004.

Conway, Flo, and Jim Siegelman. *Holy Terror: The Fundamentalist War on America's Freedoms in Religion, Politics, and Our Private Lives.* New York: Dell, 1984.

Ellis, Joseph. *Founding Brothers.* New York: Knopf, 2000.

———. *His Excellency: George Washington.* New York: Knopf, 2004.

Gage, Matilda Joslyn. *Woman, Church, & State.* Watertown, MA: Persephone Press, 1980.

Gaylor, Annie Laurie. *Women Without Superstition: "No Gods, No Masters": The Collected Writings of Women Freethinkers of the Nineteenth and Twentieth Centuries*. Madison, WI: Freedom from Religion Foundation, 1997.

——. *Woe to the Women: The Bible Tells Me So: The Bible, Female Sexuality, and the Law*. Madison, WI: Freedom from Religion Foundation, 2004, 1981, revised ed.

Harris, Sam. *The End of Faith: Religion, Terror, and the Future of Reason*. New York: W. W. Norton, 2004.

Holmes, David L. *The Faiths of the Founding Fathers*. New York: Oxford University Press, 2006.

Jacoby, Susan. *Freethinkers: A History of American Secularism*. New York: Henry Holt, 2004.

The Jefferson Bible. Boston: Beacon Press, 1989 edition.

Kaplan, Esther. *With God on Their Side*. New York: New Press, 2004.

Kimball, Charles. *When Religion Becomes Evil*. San Francisco: Harper, 2002.

Kissling, Frances, D. Maguire, M. Segers, G. Harmon, and D. Shannon. *Guide for Prochoice Catholics: The Church, the State, and Abortion Politics*. Washington, D.C.: Catholics for Free Choice, 1990.

Kramnick, Isaac, and R. Laurence Moore. *The Godless Constitution: The Case against Religious Correctness*. New York: W. W. Norton, 1996.

Levy, Leonard W. *The Establishment Clause: Religion and the First Amendment*. New York: Macmillan, 1986.

Marshall, Megan. *The Peabody Sisters*. New York: Houghton Mifflin, 2005.

McCullough, David. *John Adams*. New York: Simon & Schuster, 2001.

Meacham, Jon. *American Gospel: God, The Founding Fathers, and the Making of a Nation*. New York: Random House, 2006.

Moyers, Bill. *Moyers on America: A Journalist and His Times*. New York: Anchor, 2005.

———. "Democracy in the Balance." *Sojourners* Magazine, August 2004.

Paine, Thomas. *Common Sense*. New York, Penguin Books Great Ideas Series, 2004.

———. *The Age of Reason*. Mineola, New York: Dover, 2004.

Pfeffer, Leo. *Church State and Freedom*. Boston: Beacon Press, 1953.

Specter, Michael. "Political Science: The Bush Administration's War on the Laboratory." *New Yorker*, March 13, 2006.

Stanton, Elizabeth Cady. *The Woman's Bible*. New York: Arno. Press/A New York Times Company, 1974. Reissued ed. distributed by Quadrangle/Harper & Row.

Steiner, Franklin. *The Religious Beliefs of Our Presidents: From Washington to F.D.R.* Amherst, New York: Prometheus Books; The Freethought Library, 1995.

Treaties and Other International Acts of the United States of America, Volume 2, Documents 1–40; 1776–1818, edited by Hunter Miller. Washington, D.C.: United States Government Printing Office, 1931.

Vidal, Gore. *The American Presidency*. Cambridge, MA: South End Press, 2002.

———. *Inventing a Nation: Washington, Adams, Jefferson*. New Haven, CT: Yale University Press, 2004.

[*Note:* There are far more books and articles on the subject than space can accommodate here. I recommend a search on the subject of "separation of church and state" through the cyberstacks of amazon.com or barnesand noble.com.]

THE DECLARATION OF INDEPENDENCE
IN CONGRESS, JULY 4, 1776
THE UNANIMOUS DECLARATION OF THE THIRTEEN UNITED STATES OF AMERICA

WHEN in the Course of human Events, it becomes necessary for one People to dissolve the Political Bands which have connected them with another, and to assume among the Powers of the Earth, the separate and equal Station to which the Laws of Nature and of Nature's God entitle them, a decent Respect to the Opinions of Mankind requires that they should declare the causes which impel them to the Separation.

WE hold these Truths to be self-evident, that all Men are created equal, that they are endowed by their Creator with certain unalienable Rights, that among these are Life, Liberty and the Pursuit of Happiness—That to secure these Rights, Governments are instituted among Men, deriving their just Powers from the Consent of the Governed, that whenever any Form of Government becomes destructive of these Ends, it is the Right of the People to alter or to abolish it, and to institute new Government, laying its Foundation on such Principles, and organizing its Powers in such Form, as to them shall seem most likely to effect their Safety and Happiness. Prudence, indeed, will dictate that Governments long established should not be changed for light and transient Causes; and accordingly all Experience hath shewn, that Mankind are more disposed to suffer, while Evils are sufferable, than to right themselves by abolishing the Forms to which they are accustomed. But when a long Train of Abuses and Usurpations, pursuing invariably the same Object, evinces a Design to reduce them under absolute Despotism, it is their Right, it is their Duty, to throw off such Government, and to provide new Guards for their future Security. Such has been the patient Sufferance of these Colonies; and such is now the Necessity which constrains them to alter their former Systems of Government. The History of the present King of Great-Britain is a History of repeated Injuries and Usurpations, all having in direct Object the Establishment of an absolute Tyranny over these States. To prove this, let Facts be submitted to a candid World.

HE has refused his Assent to Laws, the most wholesome and necessary for the public Good.

HE has forbidden his Governors to pass Laws of immediate and pressing Importance, unless suspended in their Operation till his Assent should be obtained; and when so suspended, he has utterly neglected to attend to them.

HE has refused to pass other Laws for the Accommodation of large Districts of People, unless those People would relinquish the Right of Representation in the

Legislature, a Right inestimable to them, and formidable to Tyrants only.

HE has called together Legislative Bodies at Places unusual, uncomfortable, and distant from the Depository of their public Records, for the sole Purpose of fatiguing them into Compliance with his Measures.

HE has dissolved Representative Houses repeatedly, for opposing with manly Firmness his Invasions on the Rights of the People.

HE has refused for a long Time, after such Dissolutions, to cause others to be elected; whereby the Legislative Powers, incapable of the Annihilation, have returned to the People at large for their exercise; the State remaining in the mean time exposed to all the Dangers of Invasion from without, and the Convulsions within.

HE has endeavoured to prevent the Population of these States; for that Purpose obstructing the Laws for Naturalization of Foreigners; refusing to pass others to encourage their Migrations hither, and raising the Conditions of new Appropriations of Lands.

HE has obstructed the Administration of Justice, by refusing his Assent to Laws for establishing Judiciary Powers.

HE has made Judges dependent on his Will alone, for the Tenure of their Offices, and the Amount and Payment of their Salaries.

HE has erected a Multitude of new Offices, and sent hither Swarms of Officers to harrass our People, and eat out their Substance.

HE has kept among us, in Times of Peace, Standing Armies, without the consent of our Legislatures.

HE has affected to render the Military independent of and superior to the Civil Power.

HE has combined with others to subject us to a Jurisdiction foreign to our Constitution, and unacknowledged by our Laws; giving his Assent to their Acts of pretended Legislation:

FOR quartering large Bodies of Armed Troops among us;

FOR protecting them, by a mock Trial, from Punishment for any Murders which they should commit on the Inhabitants of these States:

FOR cutting off our Trade with all Parts of the World:

FOR imposing Taxes on us without our Consent:

FOR depriving us, in many Cases, of the Benefits of Trial by Jury:

FOR transporting us beyond Seas to be tried for pretended Offences:

FOR abolishing the free System of English Laws in a neighbouring Province, establishing therein an arbitrary Government, and enlarging its Boundaries, so as to render it at once an Example and fit Instrument for introducing the same absolute Rules into these Colonies:

FOR taking away our Charters, abolishing our most valuable Laws, and altering fundamentally the Forms of our Governments:

FOR suspending our own Legislatures, and declaring themselves invested with Power to legislate for us in all Cases whatsoever.

HE has abdicated Government here, by declaring us out of his Protection and waging War against us.

HE has plundered our Seas, ravaged our Coasts, burnt our Towns, and destroyed the Lives of our People.

HE is, at this Time, transporting large Armies of foreign Mercenaries to compleat the Works of Death, Desolation, and Tyranny, already begun with circumstances of Cruelty and Perfidy, scarcely paralleled in the most barbarous Ages, and totally unworthy the Head of a civilized Nation.

HE has constrained our fellow Citizens taken Captive on the high Seas to bear Arms against their Country, to become the Executioners of their Friends and Brethren, or to fall themselves by their Hands.

HE has excited domestic Insurrections amongst us, and has endeavoured to bring on the Inhabitants of our Frontiers, the merciless Indian Savages, whose known Rule of Warfare, is an undistinguished Destruction, of all Ages, Sexes and Conditions.

IN every stage of these Oppressions we have Petitioned for Redress in the most humble Terms: Our repeated Petitions have been answered only by repeated Injury. A Prince, whose Character is thus marked by every act which may define a Tyrant, is unfit to be the Ruler of a free People.

NOR have we been wanting in Attentions to our British Brethren. We have warned them from Time to Time of Attempts by their Legislature to extend an unwarrantable Jurisdiction over us. We have reminded them of the Circumstances of our Emigration and Settlement here. We have appealed to their native Justice and Magnanimity, and we have conjured them by the Ties of our common Kindred to disavow these Usurpations, which, would inevitably interrupt our Connections and Correspondence. They too have been deaf to the Voice of Justice and of Consanguinity. We must, therefore, acquiesce in the Necessity, which denounces our Separation, and hold them, as we hold the rest of Mankind, Enemies in War, in Peace, Friends.

WE, therefore, the Representatives of the UNITED STATES OF AMERICA, in GENERAL CONGRESS, Assembled, appealing to the Supreme Judge of the World for the Rectitude of our Intentions, do, in the Name, and by Authority of the good People of these Colonies, solemnly Publish and Declare, That these United Colonies are, and of Right ought to be, FREE AND INDEPENDENT STATES; that they are absolved from all Allegiance to the British Crown, and that all political Connection between them and the State of Great-Britain, is and ought to be totally dissolved; and that as FREE AND INDEPENDENT STATES, they have full Power to levy War, conclude Peace, contract Alliances, establish Commerce, and to do all other Acts and Things which INDEPENDENT STATES may of right do. And for the support of this Declaration, with a firm Reliance on the Protection of divine Providence, we mutually pledge to each other our Lives, our Fortunes, and our sacred Honor.

John Hancock.

GEORGIA, *Button Gwinnett, Lyman Hall, Geo. Walton.*

NORTH-CAROLINA, *Wm. Hooper, Joseph Hewes, John Penn.*

SOUTH-CAROLINA, *Edward Rutledge, Thos Heyward, junr., Thomas Lynch, junr., Arthur Middleton.*

MARYLAND, *Samuel Chase, Wm. Paca, Thos. Stone, Charles Carroll, of Carrollton.*

VIRGINIA, *George Wythe, Richard Henry Lee, Ths. Jefferson, Benja. Harrison, Thos. Nelson, jr., Francis Lightfoot Lee, Carter Braxton.*

PENNSYLVANIA, *Robt. Morris, Benjamin Rush, Benja. Franklin, John Morton, Geo. Clymer, Jas. Smith, Geo. Taylor, James Wilson, Geo. Ross.*

DELAWARE, *Caesar Rodney, Geo. Read.*

NEW-YORK, *Wm. Floyd, Phil. Livingston, Frank Lewis, Lewis Morris.*

NEW-JERSEY, *Richd. Stockton, Jno. Witherspoon, Fras. Hopkinson, John Hart, Abra. Clark.*

NEW-HAMPSHIRE, *Josiah Bartlett, Wm. Whipple, Matthew Thornton.*

MASSACHUSETTS-BAY, *Saml. Adams, John Adams, Robt. Treat Paine, Elbridge Gerry.*

RHODE-ISLAND AND PROVIDENCE, *C. Step. Hopkins, William Ellery.*

CONNECTICUT, *Roger Sherman, Saml. Huntington, Wm. Williams, Oliver Wolcott.*

THE CONSTITUTION OF THE
UNITED STATES OF AMERICA

We, the people of the United States, in order to form a more perfect union, establish justice, insure domestic tranquility, provide for the common defense, promote the general welfare, and secure the blessings of liberty to ourselves and our posterity, do ordain and establish this Constitution for the United States of America.

Article I

Section 1. All legislative powers herein granted shall be vested in a Congress of the United States, which shall consist of a Senate and House of Representatives.

Section 2. The House of Representatives shall be composed of members chosen every second year by the people of the several states, and the electors in each state shall have the qualifications requisite for electors of the most numerous branch of the state legislature.

No person shall be a Representative who shall not have attained to the age of twenty five years, and been seven years a citizen of the United States, and who shall not, when elected, be an inhabitant of that state in which he shall be chosen.

Representatives and direct taxes shall be apportioned among the several states which may be included within this union, according to their respective numbers, which shall be determined by adding to the whole number of free persons, including those bound to service for a term of years, and excluding Indians not taxed, three fifths of all other Persons. The actual Enumeration shall be made within three years after the first meeting of the Congress of the United States, and within every subsequent term of ten years, in such manner as they shall by law direct. The number of Representatives shall not exceed one for every thirty thousand, but each state shall have at least one Representative; and until such enumeration shall be made, the state of New Hampshire shall be entitled to chuse three, Massachusetts eight, Rhode Island and Providence Plantations one, Connecticut five, New York six, New Jersey four, Pennsylvania eight, Delaware one, Maryland six, Virginia ten, North Carolina five, South Carolina five, and Georgia three.

When vacancies happen in the Representation from any state, the executive authority thereof shall issue writs of election to fill such vacancies.

The House of Representatives shall choose their speaker and other officers; and shall have the sole power of impeachment.

Section 3. The Senate of the United States shall be composed of two Senators from each state, chosen by the legislature thereof, for six years; and each Senator shall have one vote.

Immediately after they shall be assembled in consequence of the first election, they shall be divided as equally as may be into three classes. The seats of the Senators of the first class shall be vacated at the expiration of the second year, of the second class at the expiration of the fourth year, and the third class at the expiration of the sixth year, so that one third may be chosen every second year; and if vacancies happen by resignation, or otherwise, during the recess of the legislature of any state, the executive thereof may make temporary appointments until the next meeting of the legislature, which shall then fill such vacancies.

No person shall be a Senator who shall not have attained to the age of thirty years, and been nine years a citizen of the United States and who shall not, when elected, be an inhabitant of that state for which he shall be chosen.

The Vice President of the United States shall be President of the Senate, but shall have no vote, unless they be equally divided.

The Senate shall choose their other officers, and also a President pro tempore, in the absence of the Vice President, or when he shall exercise the office of President of the United States.

The Senate shall have the sole power to try all impeachments. When sitting for that purpose, they shall be on oath or affirmation. When the President of the United States is tried, the Chief Justice shall preside: And no person shall be convicted without the concurrence of two thirds of the members present.

Judgment in cases of impeachment shall not extend further than to removal from office, and disqualification to hold and enjoy any office of honor, trust or profit under the United States: but the party convicted shall nevertheless be liable and subject to indictment, trial, judgment and punishment, according to law.

Section 4. The times, places and manner of holding elections for Senators and Representatives, shall be prescribed in each state by the legislature thereof; but the Congress may at any time by law make or alter such regulations, except as to the places of choosing Senators.

The Congress shall assemble at least once in every year, and such meeting shall be on the first Monday in December, unless they shall by law appoint a different day.

Section 5. Each House shall be the judge of the elections, returns and qualifications of its own members, and a majority of each shall constitute a quorum to do business; but a smaller number may adjourn from day to day, and may be authorized to compel the attendance of absent members, in such manner, and under such penalties as each House may provide.

Each House may determine the rules of its proceedings, punish its members for disorderly behavior, and, with the concurrence of two thirds, expel a member.

Each House shall keep a journal of its proceedings, and from time to time publish the same, excepting such parts as may in their judgment require secrecy; and the yeas and nays of the members of either House on any question shall, at the desire of one fifth of those present, be entered on the journal.

Neither House, during the session of Congress, shall, without the consent of the other, adjourn for more than three days, nor to any other place than that in which the two Houses shall be sitting.

Section 6. The Senators and Representatives shall receive a compensation for their services, to be ascertained by law, and paid out of the treasury of the United States.

They shall in all cases, except treason, felony and breach
of the peace, be privileged from arrest during their attendance at the session of their respective Houses, and in
going to and returning from the same; and for any speech
or debate in either House, they shall not be questioned in
any other place.

No Senator or Representative shall, during the time
for which he was elected, be appointed to any civil office
under the authority of the United States, which shall
have been created, or the emoluments whereof shall have
been increased during such time: and no person holding
any office under the United States, shall be a member of
either House during his continuance in office.

Section 7. All bills for raising revenue shall originate in
the House of Representatives; but the Senate may propose or concur with amendments as on other Bills.

Every bill which shall have passed the House of Representatives and the Senate, shall, before it become a law,
be presented to the President of the United States; if he
approve he shall sign it, but if not he shall return it, with
his objections to that House in which it shall have origi-
nated, who shall enter the objections at large on their
journal, and proceed to reconsider it. If after such recon-
sideration two thirds of that House shall agree to pass the
bill, it shall be sent, together with the objections, to the
other House, by which it shall likewise be reconsidered,
and if approved by two thirds of that House, it shall
become a law. But in all such cases the votes of both
Houses shall be determined by yeas and nays, and the

names of the persons voting for and against the bill shall be entered on the journal of each House respectively. If any bill shall not be returned by the President within ten days (Sundays excepted) after it shall have been presented to him, the same shall be a law, in like manner as if he had signed it, unless the Congress by their adjournment prevent its return, in which case it shall not be a law.

Every order, resolution, or vote to which the concurrence of the Senate and House of Representatives may be necessary (except on a question of adjournment) shall be presented to the President of the United States; and before the same shall take effect, shall be approved by him, or being disapproved by him, shall be repassed by two thirds of the Senate and House of Representatives, according to the rules and limitations prescribed in the case of a bill.

Section 8. The Congress shall have power to lay and collect taxes, duties, imposts and excises, to pay the debts and provide for the common defense and general welfare of the United States; but all duties, imposts and excises shall be uniform throughout the United States;

To borrow money on the credit of the United States;

To regulate commerce with foreign nations, and among the several states, and with the Indian tribes;

To establish a uniform rule of naturalization, and uniform laws on the subject of bankruptcies throughout the United States;

To coin money, regulate the value thereof, and of foreign coin, and fix the standard of weights and measures;

To provide for the punishment of counterfeiting the securities and current coin of the United States;

To establish post offices and post roads;

To promote the progress of science and useful arts, by securing for limited times to authors and inventors the exclusive right to their respective writings and discoveries;

To constitute tribunals inferior to the Supreme Court;

To define and punish piracies and felonies committed on the high seas, and offenses against the law of nations;

To declare war, grant letters of marque and reprisal, and make rules concerning captures on land and water;

To raise and support armies, but no appropriation of money to that use shall be for a longer term than two years;

To provide and maintain a navy;

To make rules for the government and regulation of the land and naval forces;

To provide for calling forth the militia to execute the laws of the union, suppress insurrections and repel invasions;

To provide for organizing, arming, and disciplining, the militia, and for governing such part of them as may be employed in the service of the United States, reserving to the states respectively, the appointment of the officers, and the authority of training the militia according to the discipline prescribed by Congress;

To exercise exclusive legislation in all cases whatsoever, over such District (not exceeding ten miles square) as may, by cession of particular states, and the acceptance of Congress, become the seat of the government of the United States, and to exercise like authority over all places purchased by the consent of the legislature of the state in which the same shall be, for the erection of forts, magazines, arsenals, dockyards, and other needful buildings; And

To make all laws which shall be necessary and proper for carrying into execution the foregoing powers, and all other powers vested by this Constitution in the government of the United States, or in any department or officer thereof.

Section 9. The migration or importation of such persons as any of the states now existing shall think proper to admit, shall not be prohibited by the Congress prior to the year one thousand eight hundred and eight, but a tax or duty may be imposed on such importation, not exceeding ten dollars for each person.

The privilege of the writ of habeas corpus shall not be suspended, unless when in cases of rebellion or invasion the public safety may require it.

No bill of attainder or ex post facto Law shall be passed.

No capitation, or other direct, tax shall be laid, unless in proportion to the census or enumeration herein before directed to be taken.

No tax or duty shall be laid on articles exported from any state.

No preference shall be given by any regulation of commerce or revenue to the ports of one state over those of another: nor shall vessels bound to, or from, one state, be obliged to enter, clear or pay duties in another.

No money shall be drawn from the treasury, but in consequence of appropriations made by law; and a regular statement and account of receipts and expenditures of all public money shall be published from time to time.

No title of nobility shall be granted by the United States: and no person holding any office of profit or trust under them, shall, without the consent of the Congress, accept of any present, emolument, office, or title, of any kind whatever, from any king, prince, or foreign state.

Section 10. No state shall enter into any treaty, alliance, or confederation; grant letters of marque and reprisal; coin money; emit bills of credit; make anything but gold and silver coin a tender in payment of debts; pass any bill of attainder, ex post facto law, or law impairing the obligation of contracts, or grant any title of nobility.

No state shall, without the consent of the Congress, lay any imposts or duties on imports or exports, except what may be absolutely necessary for executing its inspection laws: and the net produce of all duties and imposts, laid by any state on imports or exports, shall be for the use of the treasury of the United States; and all such laws shall be subject to the revision and control of the Congress.

No state shall, without the consent of Congress, lay any duty of tonnage, keep troops, or ships of war in time of peace, enter into any agreement or compact with another state, or with a foreign power, or engage in war, unless actually invaded, or in such imminent danger as will not admit of delay.

Article II

Section 1. The executive power shall be vested in a President of the United States of America. He shall hold his office during the term of four years, and, together with the Vice President, chosen for the same term, be elected, as follows:

Each state shall appoint, in such manner as the Legislature thereof may direct, a number of electors, equal to the whole number of Senators and Representatives to which the State may be entitled in the Congress: but no Senator or Representative, or person holding an office of trust or profit under the United States, shall be appointed an elector.

The electors shall meet in their respective states, and vote by ballot for two persons, of whom one at least shall not be an inhabitant of the same state with themselves. And they shall make a list of all the persons voted for, and of the number of votes for each; which list they shall sign and certify, and transmit sealed to the seat of the government of the United States, directed to the President of the Senate. The President of the Senate shall, in the presence of the Senate and House of Representatives, open all the certificates, and the votes shall then be counted. The person having the greatest number of votes shall be the President, if such number be a majority of the whole number of electors appointed; and if there be more than one who have such majority, and have an equal number of votes, then the House of Representatives shall immediately choose by ballot one of them for President; and if no person have a majority, then from the five highest on the list the said House shall in like manner choose the President. But in choosing the President, the votes shall be taken by States, the representation from each state having one vote; A quorum for this purpose shall consist of a member or members from two thirds of the states, and a majority of all the states shall be necessary to a choice. In every case, after the choice of the President, the person having the greatest number of votes of the electors shall be the Vice President. But if there should remain two or more who have equal votes, the Senate shall choose from them by ballot the Vice President.

The Congress may determine the time of choosing the electors, and the day on which they shall give their votes; which day shall be the same throughout the United States.

No person except a natural born citizen, or a citizen of the United States, at the time of the adoption of this Constitution, shall be eligible to the office of President; neither shall any person be eligible to that office who shall not have attained to the age of thirty five years, and been fourteen Years a resident within the United States.

In case of the removal of the President from office, or of his death, resignation, or inability to discharge the powers and duties of the said office, the same shall devolve on the Vice President, and the Congress may by law provide for the case of removal, death, resignation or inability, both of the President and Vice President, declaring what officer shall then act as President, and such officer shall act accordingly, until the disability be removed, or a President shall be elected.

The President shall, at stated times, receive for his services, a compensation, which shall neither be increased nor diminished during the period for which he shall have been elected, and he shall not receive within that period any other emolument from the United States, or any of them.

Before he enter on the execution of his office, he shall take the following oath or affirmation: "I do solemnly swear (or affirm) that I will faithfully execute the office of President of the United States, and will to the best of my ability, preserve, protect and defend the Constitution of the United States."

Section 2. The President shall be commander in chief of the Army and Navy of the United States, and of the militia of the several states, when called into the actual service of the United States; he may require the opinion, in writing, of the principal officer in each of the executive departments, upon any subject relating to the duties of their respective offices, and he shall have power to grant reprieves and pardons for offenses against the United States, except in cases of impeachment.

He shall have power, by and with the advice and consent of the Senate, to make treaties, provided two thirds of the Senators present concur; and he shall nominate, and by and with the advice and consent of the Senate, shall appoint ambassadors, other public ministers and consuls, judges of the Supreme Court, and all other officers of the United States, whose appointments are not herein otherwise provided for, and which shall be established by law: but the Congress may by law vest the appointment of such inferior officers, as they think proper, in the President alone, in the courts of law, or in the heads of departments.

The President shall have power to fill up all vacancies that may happen during the recess of the Senate, by granting commissions which shall expire at the end of their next session.

Section 3. He shall from time to time give to the Congress information of the state of the union, and recommend to their consideration such measures as he shall judge necessary and expedient; he may, on extraordinary occasions, convene both Houses, or either of them, and in case of disagreement between them, with respect to the time of adjournment, he may adjourn them to such time as he shall think proper; he shall receive ambassadors and other public ministers; he shall take care that the laws be faithfully executed, and shall commission all the officers of the United States.

Section 4. The President, Vice President and all civil officers of the United States, shall be removed from office on impeachment for, and conviction of, treason, bribery, or other high crimes and misdemeanors.

Article III

Section 1. The judicial power of the United States shall be vested in one Supreme Court, and in such inferior courts as the Congress may from time to time ordain and establish. The judges, both of the supreme and inferior courts, shall hold their offices during good behaviour, and shall, at stated times, receive for their services, a compensation, which shall not be diminished during their continuance in office.

Section 2. The judicial power shall extend to all cases, in law and equity, arising under this Constitution, the laws of the United States, and treaties made, or which shall be made, under their authority; to all cases affecting ambassadors, other public ministers and consuls; to all cases of admiralty and maritime jurisdiction; to controversies to which the United States shall be a party; to controversies between two or more states; between a state and citizens of another state; between citizens of different states; between citizens of the same state claiming lands under grants of different states, and between a state, or the citizens thereof, and foreign states, citizens or subjects.

In all cases affecting ambassadors, other public ministers and consuls, and those in which a state shall be party, the Supreme Court shall have original jurisdiction. In all the other cases before mentioned, the Supreme Court shall have appellate jurisdiction, both as to law and fact, with such exceptions, and under such regulations as the Congress shall make.

The trial of all crimes, except in cases of impeachment, shall be by jury; and such trial shall be held in the state where the said crimes shall have been committed; but when not committed within any state, the trial shall be at such place or places as the Congress may by law have directed.

Section 3. Treason against the United States, shall consist only in levying war against them, or in adhering to their enemies, giving them aid and comfort. No person shall be convicted of treason unless on the testimony of two witnesses to the same overt act, or on confession in open court.

The Congress shall have power to declare the punishment of treason, but no attainder of treason shall work corruption of blood, or forfeiture except during the life of the person attainted.

Article IV

Section 1. Full faith and credit shall be given in each state to the public acts, records, and judicial proceedings of every other state. And the Congress may by general laws prescribe the manner in which such acts, records, and proceedings shall be proved, and the effect thereof.

Section 2. The citizens of each state shall be entitled to all privileges and immunities of citizens in the several states.

A person charged in any state with treason, felony, or other crime, who shall flee from justice, and be found in another state, shall on demand of the executive authority of the state from which he fled, be delivered up, to be removed to the state having jurisdiction of the crime.

No person held to service or labor in one state, under the laws thereof, escaping into another, shall, in consequence of any law or regulation therein, be discharged from such service or labor, but shall be delivered up on claim of the party to whom such service or labor may be due.

Section 3. New states may be admitted by the Congress into this union; but no new states shall be formed or erected within the jurisdiction of any other state; nor any state be formed by the junction of two or more states, or parts of states, without the consent of the legislatures of the states concerned as well as of the Congress.

The Congress shall have power to dispose of and make all needful rules and regulations respecting the territory or other property belonging to the United States; and nothing in this Constitution shall be so construed as to prejudice any claims of the United States, or of any particular state.

Section 4. The United States shall guarantee to every state in this union a republican form of government, and shall protect each of them against invasion; and on application of the legislature, or of the executive (when the legislature cannot be convened) against domestic violence.

Article V

The Congress, whenever two thirds of both houses shall deem it necessary, shall propose amendments to this Constitution, or, on the application of the legislatures of two thirds of the several states, shall call a convention for proposing amendments, which, in either case, shall be valid to all intents and purposes, as part of this Constitution, when ratified by the legislatures of three fourths of the several states, or by conventions in three fourths thereof, as the one or the other mode of ratification may be proposed by the Congress; provided that no amendment which may be made prior to the year one thousand eight hundred and eight shall in any manner affect the first and fourth clauses in the ninth section of the first article; and that no state, without its consent, shall be deprived of its equal suffrage in the Senate.

Article VI

All debts contracted and engagements entered into, before the adoption of this Constitution, shall be as valid against the United States under this Constitution, as under the Confederation.

This Constitution, and the laws of the United States which shall be made in pursuance thereof; and all treaties made, or which shall be made, under the authority of the United States, shall be the supreme law of the land; and the judges in every state shall be bound thereby, anything in the Constitution or laws of any State to the contrary notwithstanding.

The Senators and Representatives before mentioned, and the members of the several state legislatures, and all executive and judicial officers, both of the United States and of the several states, shall be bound by oath or affirmation, to support this Constitution; but no religious test shall ever be required as a qualification to any office or public trust under the United States.

Article VII

The ratification of the conventions of nine states shall be sufficient for the establishment of this Constitution between the states so ratifying the same.

Done in convention by the unanimous consent of the states present the seventeenth day of September in the year of our Lord one thousand seven hundred and eighty seven and of the independence of the United States of America the twelfth. In witness whereof We have hereunto subscribed our Names,

G. Washington-Presidt. and deputy from Virginia
New Hampshire: John Langdon, Nicholas Gilman
Massachusetts: Nathaniel Gorham, Rufus King
Connecticut: Wm: Saml. Johnson, Roger Sherman
New York: Alexander Hamilton
New Jersey: Wil: Livingston, David Brearly, Wm. Paterson, Jona: Dayton
Pennsylvania: B. Franklin, Thomas Mifflin, Robt. Morris, Geo. Clymer, Thos. FitzSimons, Jared Ingersoll, James Wilson, Gouv Morris
Delaware: Geo: Read, Gunning Bedford jun, John Dickinson, Richard Bassett, Jaco: Broom
Maryland: James McHenry, Dan of St Thos. Jenifer, Danl Carroll
Virginia: John Blair—, James Madison Jr.
North Carolina: Wm. Blount, Richd. Dobbs Spaight, Hu Williamson
South Carolina: J. Rutledge, Charles Cotesworth Pinckney, Charles Pinckney, Pierce Butler
Georgia: William Few, Abr Baldwin

THE BILL OF RIGHTS AND LATER AMENDMENTS TO THE CONSTITUTION
THE BILL OF RIGHTS: AMENDMENTS 1–10

U. S. Congress, at the City of New York, March 4, 1789.
The Conventions of a number of the States having, at the time of adopting the Constitution, expressed a desire, in order to prevent misconstruction or abuse of its powers, that further declaratory and restrictive clauses should be added, and as extending the ground of public confidence in the Government will best insure the beneficent ends of its institution;

Resolved, by the Senate and House of Representatives of the United States of America, in Congress assembled, two-thirds of both Houses concurring, that the following articles be proposed to the Legislatures of the several States, as amendments to the Constitution of the United States; all or any of which articles, when ratified by three-fourths of the said Legislatures, to be valid to all intents and purposes as part of the said Constitution, namely:

Amendment I

Congress shall make no law respecting an establishment of religion, or prohibiting the free exercise thereof; or abridging the freedom of speech, or of the press; or the right of the people peaceably to assemble, and to petition the government for a redress of grievances.

Amendment II

A well regulated militia being necessary to the security of

a free state, the right of the people to keep and bear arms, shall not be infringed.

Amendment III

No soldier shall, in time of peace be quartered in any house, without the consent of the owner, nor in time of war, but in a manner to be prescribed by law.

Amendment IV

The right of the people to be secure in their persons, houses, papers, and effects, against unreasonable searches and seizures, shall not be violated, and no warrants shall issue, but upon probable cause, supported by oath or affirmation, and particularly describing the place to be searched, and the persons or things to be seized.

Amendment V

No person shall be held to answer for a capital, or otherwise infamous crime, unless on a presentment or indictment of a grand jury, except in cases arising in the land or naval forces, or in the militia, when in actual service in time of war or public danger; nor shall any person be subject for the same offense to be twice put in jeopardy of life or limb; nor shall be compelled in any criminal case to be a witness against himself, nor be deprived of life, liberty, or property, without due process of law; nor shall private property be taken for public use, without just compensation.

Amendment VI

In all criminal prosecutions, the accused shall enjoy the right to a speedy and public trial, by an impartial jury of the state and district wherein the crime shall have been committed, which district shall have been previously ascertained by law, and to be informed of the nature and cause of the accusation; to be confronted with the witnesses against him; to have compulsory process for obtaining witnesses in his favor, and to have the assistance of counsel for his defense.

Amendment VII

In suits at common law, where the value in controversy shall exceed twenty dollars, the right of trial by jury shall be preserved, and no fact tried by a jury, shall be otherwise reexamined in any court of the United States, than according to the rules of the common law.

Amendment VIII

Excessive bail shall not be required, nor excessive fines imposed, nor cruel and unusual punishments inflicted.

Amendment IX

The enumeration in the Constitution, of certain rights, shall not be construed to deny or disparage others retained by the people.

Amendment X

The powers not delegated to the United States by the Constitution, nor prohibited by it to the states, are reserved to the states respectively, or to the people.

LATER AMENDMENTS TO THE U.S. CONSTITUTION

Amendment XI

The Judicial power of the United States shall not be construed to extend to any suit in law or equity, commenced or prosecuted against one of the United States by Citizens of another State, or by Citizens or Subjects of any Foreign State.

Amendment XII

The Electors shall meet in their respective states, and vote by ballot for President and Vice-President, one of whom, at least, shall not be an inhabitant of the same state with themselves; they shall name in their ballots the person voted for as President, and in distinct ballots the person voted for as Vice-President, and they shall make distinct lists of all persons voted for as President, and of all persons voted for as Vice-President, and of the number of votes for each, which lists they shall sign and certify, and transmit sealed to the seat of the government of the United States, directed to the President of the Senate;—The President of the Senate shall, in the presence of the Senate and House of Representatives, open all the certificates and the votes shall then be counted;—The person having the greatest number of votes for President, shall be the President, if such number be a majority of the whole number of Electors appointed; and if no person have such majority, then from the persons having the highest numbers not exceeding three on the list of those voted for as President, the House of Representatives shall choose immediately, by ballot, the President. But in choosing the President, the votes shall be taken by states, the representation from each state having one vote; a quorum for this purpose shall consist of a member or members from two-thirds of the states, and a majority of all the states shall be necessary to a choice. And if the House of Representatives shall not choose a President whenever the right of choice shall devolve upon them, before the fourth day of March next following, then the Vice-President shall act as President, as in the case of the death or other constitutional disability of the President.— The person having the greatest number of votes as Vice-President, shall be the Vice-President, if such number be a majority of the whole number of Electors appointed, and if no person have a majority, then from the two highest numbers on the list, the Senate shall choose the Vice-President; a quorum for the purpose shall consist of two-thirds of the whole number of Senators, and a majority of the whole number shall be necessary to a choice. But no person constitutionally ineligible to the office of President shall be eligible to that of Vice-President of the United States.

Amendment XIII

Section 1. Neither slavery nor involuntary servitude, except as a punishment for crime whereof the party shall have been duly convicted, shall exist within the United States, or any place subject to their jurisdiction.

Section 2. Congress shall have power to enforce this article by appropriate legislation.

Amendment XIV

Section 1. All persons born or naturalized in the United States, and subject to the jurisdiction thereof, are citizens of the United States and of the State wherein they reside. No State shall make or enforce any law which shall abridge the privileges or immunities of citizens of the United States; nor shall any State deprive any person of life, liberty, or property, without due process of law; nor deny to any person within its jurisdiction the equal protection of the laws.

Section 2. Representatives shall be apportioned among the several States according to their respective numbers, counting the whole number of persons in each State, excluding Indians not taxed. But when the right to vote at any election for the choice of electors for President and Vice President of the United States, Representatives in Congress, the Executive and Judicial officers of a State, or the members of the Legislature thereof, is denied to any of the male inhabitants of such State, being twenty-one years of age, and citizens of the United States, or in any way abridged, except for participation in rebellion, or other crime, the basis of representation therein shall be reduced in the proportion which the number of such male citizens shall bear to the whole number of male citizens twenty-one years of age in such State.

Section 3. No person shall be a Senator or Representative in Congress, or elector of President and Vice President, or hold any office, civil or military, under the United States, or under any State, who, having previously taken an oath, as a member of Congress, or as an officer of the United States, or as a member of any State legislature, or as an executive or judicial officer of any State, to support the Constitution of the United States, shall have engaged in insurrection or rebellion against the same, or given aid or comfort to the enemies thereof. But Congress may by a vote of two-thirds of each House, remove such disability.

Section 4. The validity of the public debt of the United States, authorized by law, including debts incurred for payment of pensions and bounties for services in suppressing insurrection or rebellion, shall not be questioned. But neither the United States nor any State shall assume or pay any debt or obligation incurred in aid of insurrection or rebellion against the United States, or any claim for the loss or emancipation of any slave; but all such debts, obligations and claims shall be held illegal and void.

Section 5. The Congress shall have power to enforce, by appropriate legislation, the provisions of this article.

Amendment XV

Section 1. The right of citizens of the United States to vote shall not be denied or abridged by the United States or by any State on account of race, color, or previous condition of servitude.

Section 2. The Congress shall have power to enforce this article by appropriate legislation.

Amendment XVI

The Congress shall have power to lay and collect taxes on incomes, from whatever source derived, without apportionment among the several States, and without regard to any census or enumeration.

Amendment XVII

The Senate of the United States shall be composed of two Senators from each State, elected by the people thereof, for six years; and each Senator shall have one vote. The electors in each State shall have the qualifications requisite for electors of the most numerous branch of the State legislatures.

When vacancies happen in the representation of any State in the Senate, the executive authority of such State shall issue writs of election to fill such vacancies: *Provided,* That the legislature of any State may empower the executive thereof to make temporary appointments until the people fill the vacancies by election as the legislature may direct.

This amendment shall not be so construed as to affect the election or term of any Senator chosen before it becomes valid as part of the Constitution.

Amendment XVIII

Section 1. After one year from the ratification of this article the manufacture, sale, or transportation of intoxicating liquors within, the importation thereof into, or the exportation thereof from the United States and all territory subject to the jurisdiction thereof for beverage purposes is hereby prohibited.

Section 2. The Congress and the several States shall have concurrent power to enforce this article by appropriate legislation.

Section 3. This article shall be inoperative unless it shall have been ratified as an amendment to the Constitution by the legislatures of the several States, as provided in the Constitution, within seven years from the date of the submission hereof to the States by the Congress.

Amendment XIX

The right of citizens of the United States to vote shall not be denied or abridged by the United States or by any State on account of sex.

Congress shall have power to enforce this article by appropriate legislation.

Amendment XX

Section 1. The terms of the President and Vice President shall end at noon on the 20th day of January, and the terms of Senators and Representatives at noon on the 3d day of January, of the years in which such terms would have ended if this article had not been ratified; and the terms of their successors shall then begin.

Section 2. The Congress shall assemble at least once in every year, and such meeting shall begin at noon on the 3d day of January, unless they shall by law appoint a different day.

Section 3. If, at the time fixed for the beginning of the term of the President, the President elect shall have died, the Vice President elect shall become President. If a President shall not have been chosen before the time fixed for the beginning of his term, or if the President elect shall have failed to qualify, then the Vice President elect shall act as President until a President shall have qualified; and the Congress may by law provide for the case wherein neither a President elect nor a Vice President elect shall have qualified, declaring who shall then act as President, or the manner in which one who is to act shall be selected, and such person shall act accordingly until a President or Vice President shall have qualified.

Section 4. The Congress may by law provide for the case of the death of any of the persons from whom the House of Representatives may choose a President whenever the right of choice shall have devolved upon them, and for the case of the death of any of the persons from whom the Senate may choose a Vice President whenever the right of choice shall have devolved upon them.

Section 5. Sections 1 and 2 shall take effect on the 15th day of October following the ratification of this article.

Section 6. This article shall be inoperative unless it shall have been ratified as an amendment to the Constitution by the legislatures of three-fourths of the several States within seven years from the date of its submission.

Amendment XXI

Section 1. The eighteenth article of amendment to the Constitution of the United States is hereby repealed.

Section 2. The transportation or importation into any State, Territory, or possession of the United States for delivery or use therein of intoxicating liquors, in violation of the laws thereof, is hereby prohibited.

Section 3. This article shall be inoperative unless it shall have been ratified as an amendment to the Constitution by conventions in the several States, as provided in the Constitution, within seven years from the date of the submission hereof to the States by the Congress.

Amendment XXII

Section 1. No person shall be elected to the office of the President more than twice, and no person who has held the office of President, or acted as President, for more than two years of a term to which some other person was elected President shall be elected to the office of the President more than once. But this Article shall not apply to any person holding the office of President when this Article was proposed by the Congress, and shall not prevent any person who may be holding the office of President, or acting as President, during the term within which this Article becomes operative from holding the office of President or acting as President during the remainder of such term.

Section 2. This article shall be inoperative unless it shall have been ratified as an amendment to the Constitution by the legislatures of three-fourths of the several States within seven years from the date of its submission to the States by the Congress.

Amendment XXIII

Section 1. The District constituting the seat of Government of the United States shall appoint in such manner as the Congress may direct: A number of electors of President and Vice President equal to the whole number of Senators and Representatives in Congress to which the District would be entitled if it were a State, but in no event more than the least populous State; they shall be in addition to those appointed by the States, but they shall be considered, for the purposes of the election of President and Vice President, to be electors appointed by a State;

and they shall meet in the District and perform such duties as provided by the twelfth article of amendment.

Section 2. The Congress shall have power to enforce this article by appropriate legislation.

Amendment XXIV

Section 1. The right of citizens of the United States to vote in any primary or other election for President or Vice President, for electors for President or Vice President, or for Senator or Representative in Congress, shall not be denied or abridged by the United States or any State by reason of failure to pay any poll tax or other tax.

Section 2. The Congress shall have power to enforce this article by appropriate legislation.

Amendment XXV

Section 1. In case of the removal of the President from office or of his death or resignation, the Vice President shall become President.

Section 2. Whenever there is a vacancy in the office of the Vice President, the President shall nominate a Vice President who shall take office upon confirmation by a majority vote of both Houses of Congress.

Section 3. Whenever the President transmits to the President pro tempore of the Senate and the Speaker of the House of Representatives his written declaration that he is unable to discharge the powers and duties of his office, and until he transmits to them a written declaration to the contrary, such powers and duties shall be discharged by the Vice President as Acting President.

Section 4. Whenever the Vice President and a majority

of either the principal officers of the executive departments or of such other body as Congress may by law provide, transmit to the President pro tempore of the Senate
and the Speaker of the House of Representatives their
written declaration that the President is unable to discharge the powers and duties of his office, the Vice President shall immediately assume the powers and duties of
the office as Acting President.

Thereafter, when the President transmits to the President pro tempore of the Senate and the Speaker of the
House of Representatives his written declaration that no
inability exists, he shall resume the powers and duties of
his office unless the Vice President and a majority of either
the principal officers of the executive department or of
such other body as Congress may by law provide, transmit
within four days to the President pro tempore of the
Senate and the Speaker of the House of Representatives
their written declaration that the President is unable to
discharge the powers and duties of his office. Thereupon
Congress shall decide the issue, assembling within forty-
eight hours for that purpose if not in session. If the Congress, within twenty-one days after receipt of the latter
written declaration, or, if Congress is not in session, within
twenty-one days after Congress is required to assemble,
determines by two-thirds vote of both Houses that the
President is unable to discharge the powers and duties of
his office, the Vice President shall continue to discharge
the same as Acting President; otherwise, the President
shall resume the powers and duties of his office.

Amendment XXVI

Section 1. The right of citizens of the United States, who are eighteen years of age or older, to vote shall not be denied or abridged by the United States or by any State on account of age.

Section 2. The Congress shall have power to enforce this article by appropriate legislation.

Amendment XXVII

No law, varying the compensation for the services of the Senators and Representatives, shall take effect, until an election of Representatives shall have intervened.